The Compact Guide

Step by Step
Crochet Gifts

The Compact Guide

Step by Step Crochet Gifts

Welcome...

Step by Step Crochet Gifts is the perfect companion for crochet crafters of any skill level who are looking to create adorable gifts for all the family to enjoy. From baby toys and playroom characters to cosy jumpers and cute dresses, there really is something for everyone. With easy-to-follow instructions and straightforward patterns, you'll be making unique presents and clothes for all your loved ones. So, what are you waiting for?

Turn the page and start your creative journey today!

First published in the UK 2021 by Sona Books
an imprint of Danann Media Publishing Ltd.

Editor for Danann Tom O'Neill

Images courtesy of:
Jayne Jackson; Karen Penroz on Unsplash;

CAT NO: SON0504
ISBN: 978-1-915343-99-4
Made in the UAE.

Contents

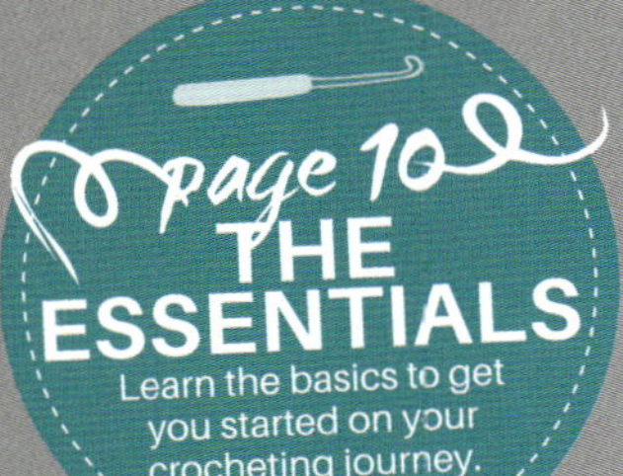

page 10
THE ESSENTIALS
Learn the basics to get you started on your crocheting journey.

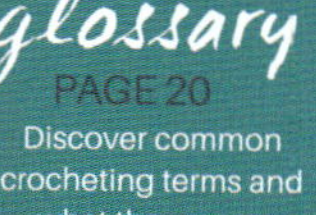

glossary
PAGE 20
Discover common crocheting terms and what they mean

Baby

26
Rainbow rattle

30
Lamb lovey

34
Hushabye sleeping bag

38
Koala teether and rattle

42
Hot air balloon mobile

46
Sherbet stripes blanket

Playroom

50
Fox puppet

54
Amigurumi food

60
Sleepy sheep

62
Little dress-up doll

66
Octopus hand puppet

70
Giant mouse

74
Football captain

78
Horace the monster

82
Little bunny

84
Trio of dinosaurs

94
Gelato rainbow basket

98
Ripples wall hanging

Clothes

102
Summer diamonds toddler dress

106
Rainbow scarf

108
Snappy slippers

112
Cosy cobbles earwarmer

114
Horizon jumper

120
Crossed stitch fingerless gloves

124
Find-your-rhythm beanie

128
Pyjama-eating elephant

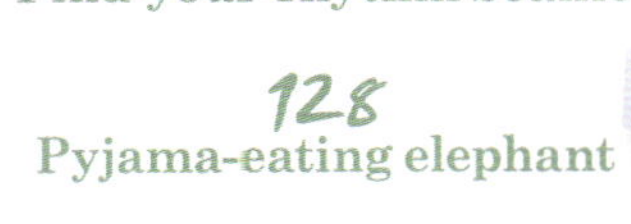

The essentials

Learn the basics to get you started on your crocheting journey

HOLDING YOUR HOOK

OVERHAND (KNIFE GRIP)
This technique is also known as the knife grip, as you grip the crochet hook as if you're holding a knife. Place your hand over the hook, then support the handle in your chosen palm.

UNDERHAND (PENCIL GRIP)
For this technique, hold the hook like a pencil (hence the name pencil grip). Hold the thumb rest between your thumb and index finger and then let the handle rest on top of your hand.

HOLDING YOUR YARN

THE LOOSE-YARN HOLD
Holding the end of the yarn in your right hand and with your left palm facing you, weave the yarn in front of your little finger, behind your ring finger, in front of your middle finger and behind your index finger.

THE PINKY HOLD
Looping the yarn once around your little finger may help you to keep a secure grip. Follow the instructions for the loose-yarn hold, but begin by looping the yarn around your little finger clockwise.

MAKE A SLIPKNOT

MAKE A LOOP
Wrap the yarn once around two of your fingers on your left hand to form a loop, making sure to leave a tail of at least 10cm (or longer if your pattern calls for it).

DRAW UP A LOOP
Take the loop off the hook and grip between your thumb and fingers. Insert your hook from right to left, catch the working yarn and pull through to make a loop on your hook.

PULL TO CLOSE THE LOOP
Grip the tail and the working yarn and pull them tight to form a knot. Pull the working yarn to tighten the loop around your hook. It needs to be able to move up and down your hook so don't pull too tight.

CHAIN STITCH (CH)

YARN OVER & DRAW UP LOOP
Starting with a slipknot, move your hook underneath your yarn and pull this through the loop already on your hook.

KEEP GOING
Keep going to create a chain of the length needed in your pattern. Try not to make the stitches too tight as this will make it difficult when working subsequent rows. Keep the stitches even or you will get an uneven edge on your piece.

COUNTING CHAINS

To count the chains, identify the Vs on the side that's facing you. Each of these is one chain. The V above the slipknot is your first chain, but don't count the loop on your hook. This is the working loop and does not count as a chain. If you are creating a very long chain, it might help to mark every 10 or 20 stitches with a stitch marker.

SLIPSTICH (SS/SL ST)

INTO CHAIN
Insert your hook into the second chain from the hook. Yarn over (yo). Pull your hook back through the chain. There should be two loops on your hook.

PULL THROUGH
Avoiding the urge to yarn over, continue to pull the yarn through the second loop on the hook. You have completed the stitch and should have one loop on your hook.

All the tutorials in this book can be followed by left-handed crocheters. Simply reverse the instructions and hold the picture tutorials up to a mirror to see how you should be working. So every time you see 'Right' replace it with 'Left' and every time you see 'Clockwise' replace with 'Counterclockwise' (and vice versa)

WORKING THE FOUNDATION CHAIN

FRONT OF THE CHAIN
Looking at the front side of your chain, you will see a row of sideways Vs, each with two loops - a top loop and a bottom loop.

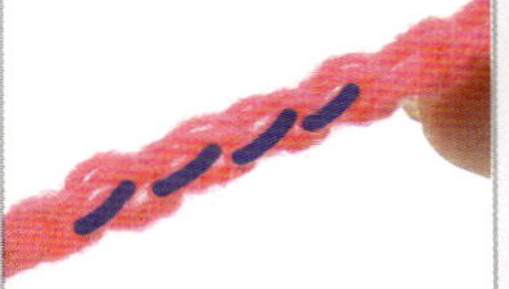

BACK OF THE CHAIN
When you look at the back side of the chain, you will see a line of bumps in between the loops. These are called the back bumps.

METHOD 1: TOP LOOP
For this method, hook under the top loop only.

2

METHOD 2: TOP TWO LOOPS
Hooking under both the top loop and the back bump is sometimes referred to as the top two loops of the chain.

METHOD 3: TOP LOOP AND BACK BUMP
Turn over your chain so that the back bumps are facing you. Insert your hook under the back bump.

It doesn't matter which method you use as long as you are consistent when moving along the chain. Working under the top loop is the easiest method for beginners, but does not create as neat an edge as working under the back bumps.

UK and US terms

Confusingly, patterns can follow either UK or US naming conventions. To make things even more difficult, the same name is used to mean different stitches under either convention. Most patterns will state whether they are using US or UK terminology, but if not, checking the pattern's country of origin may be a good place to start. A handy trick to remember is that there is no stitch called a single crochet (sc) in UK terminology, so if you see this on the pattern, then you know it is using US naming conventions.
All patterns in this book use UK terminology.

UK	US
Chain (ch)	Chain (ch)
Double crochet (dc)	Single crochet (sc)
Treble crochet (tr)	Double crochet (dc)
Half treble crochet (htr)	Half double crochet (hdc)
Double treble crochet (dtr)	Triple (treble) crochet (tr)
Slip stitch (sl st/ss)	Slip stitch (sl st/ss)

DOUBLE CROCHET (DC)

INSERT HOOK
Working into your foundation chain, identify the second chain from your hook and then insert your hook.

DRAW UP A LOOP
Yarn over (yo), then draw up a loop. You will now have two loops on your crochet hook.

PULL TO CLOSE THE LOOP
Yarn over and then draw the yarn through both loops on the hook so you have one loop left on your hook. You have now completed the stitch.

TREBLE CROCHET (TR)

INSERT HOOK
Working into your foundation chain, identify the fourth chain from your hook. Make a yarn over (yo) and then insert your hook into the fourth chain from the hook.

YARN OVER AND DRAW UP A LOOP
Yarn over, then draw up a loop. There should now be three loops on your hook.

YARN OVER AND DRAW UP A LOOP
Yarn over, then draw the yarn through two of the loops on your hook. There should now be two loops on your hook.

COMPLETE THE STITCH
Yarn over and then draw the yarn through the two loops left on the hook. You have completed the stitch and should have one loop on your hook.

DOUBLE TREBLE CROCHET (DTR)

MAKE A LOOP
Working into your foundation chain, identify the fifth chain from your hook. Yarn over twice and insert your hook into the fifth chain from the hook. Yarn over and draw up a loop. There should be four loops on your hook. Yarn over, then draw the yarn through two of the loops on your hook. There should now be three loops on your hook.

DRAW UP A LOOP
Yarn over, then draw the yarn through two of the loops on your hook again. There should now be two loops on your hook. Yarn over, then draw the yarn through the two loops on your hook. There should now be one loop on your hook.
You have completed the stitch.

HALF TREBLE CROCHET (HTR)

INSERT HOOK
Working into your foundation chain, identify the third chain from your hook. Make a yarn over (yo) and then insert your hook into the third chain from the hook.

YARN OVER AND DRAW UP A LOOP
Yarn over, then draw up a loop. There should now be three loops on your hook. Yarn over, then draw the yarn through all three loops on your hook. The stitch is now complete and there should be one loop on your hook.

IDENTIFYING STITCHES

There are two ways to count stitches: either by counting the Vs along the top of the work or by counting the posts. If you count the Vs, make sure you never count the loop that is on your hook. When counting either Vs or posts, you must take careful consideration when you come to the turning chain. If it is counted as a stitch in your pattern, then count it, but if not, leave it out.

UNDER BOTH

Hooking under the front and back loops of the stitch is the most common way to work into a row. Use this method unless told otherwise.

INSERT YOUR HOOK

After the turning chain, insert your hook so that it goes in under both the front and back loops of the V.

FRONT AND BACK LOOPS ONLY (FLO AND BLO)

Sometimes a pattern will say to work into Front or Back loops only. Doing so will create ridges in your work, for example, you may use FLO/BLO to add ribbing to a hat. To work into Front loops only (FLO) identify the loop closest to you and work into the stitch as normal. For Back loops, use the loop farthest away from you.

JOIN A NEW YARN

THE LAST STITCH

When you think you don't have enough yarn left in your current ball, or you need to change colour, begin the last stitch of your current row with the old yarn, but stop before you reach the final step (yo and draw through all loops on hook).

DRAW UP A LOOP

Make a yarn over (yo) with the new ball of yarn and complete the stitch. Leave a tail of at least a 15cm (5.9in) on the new yarn. Continue crocheting with the new yarn, and drop the old yarn. You can hide the ends in the inside of your project.

CHANGING COLOUR

ALONG THE EDGE

When you're creating stripes by changing colour at the beginning of every row or so, you can leave the unworked yarn dangling at the edge. This way you can pick it up again when you need to. To do this, carry it loosely up the edge of the work in order to begin your new row. Adding an edge or border will hide the carried yarn strands.

OVER THE TOP OF THE OLD YARN

If you need to change colours regularly and mid-row, crocheting over the top of the yarn you're not currently using is a good way to keep it concealed and eliminates ends that would need weaving in. This technique is great when you are creating a reversible fabric, as it keeps both sides looking neat.

FLOATING STRANDS

If only one side of your final product will be seen, then you can carry the unused colours along the back of the work.Just drop the yarn you're not using, then pick it up again when you need it, loosely bringing it across the back of the work. This works best if the strands are only a few stitches long. If they are longer, cut the threads and weave in instead.

CUTTING THE YARN

If you are putting in a big block of one colour, it's best to cut the yarn and treat it like you're joining a new yarn, then weave in the ends of the yarn at a later stage.

TURNING CHAINS

Whenever you turn your work, you will need to create a turning chain to start your next row. When using anything but double crochet, the turning chain always counts as the first stitch (unless specified otherwise), and the next stitch should be created in the second stitch from the hook. Different stitches need different heights of turning chains, to match the height of the stitch about to be made.

Stitch (UK)	Number of turning chain sts
Double crochet (dc)	1
Half-treble crochet (htr)	2
Treble crochet (tr)	3
Double treble crochet (dtr)	4

INCREASE

INCREASING IN THE MIDDLE OF A ROW (TREBLES AS EXAMPLE)

Make a treble crochet in the next stitch. Make another treble crochet in the same stitch. You have increased your stitch count by one.

INCREASING AT THE START OF A ROW

As the turning chain normally counts as a stitch (except in dc), increasing at the start of a row is different. To increase, insert your hook into the first stitch at the base of the chain and make the stitch. The stitch you've just made and the turning chain count as two stitches, and you have made an increase.

DECREASE

DOUBLE CROCHET TWO STITCHES TOGETHER (DC2TOG)

Insert your hook into the next stitch, as if to make a double crochet. Draw up a loop. Without completing the stitch, insert your hook into the next stitch as if to make another double crochet. Draw up a loop. You should now have three loops on your hook. Yarn over (yo) and draw the loop through all three stitches on your hook. Having worked into two stitches, but only created one, you have decreased by one.

TREBLE CROCHET THREE STITCHES TOGETHER (TR3TOG)

Yarn over and insert your hook into the next stitch, as if to make a treble crochet. Draw up a loop, yarn over and draw through two loops on the hook. There should now be two loops on your hook. *Without completing the stitch, yarn over and insert your hook into the next stitch. Draw up a loop, yarn over and draw through two loops on the hook.* There should now be three loops on your hook. Repeat * to * into the next stitch. There should now be four loops on your hook, yarn over and draw the yarn through all four loops to complete the decrease.

STARTING IN THE ROUND

METHOD 1: SINGLE CHAIN START

Chain two. Now make a double crochet (dc) into the second chain from your hook. Make the rest of your doubles into the same chain stitch as your first double crochet.

METHOD 2: MULTIPLE CHAIN START

Make a short chain, depending on the pattern that you're following. Here we have shown five chains. Create a slip stitch (sl st) into the first chain that you created. Work your first round into the middle of the ring you have just made. Now either continue to work in a spiral or connect the last double crochet to the first with a slip stitch, create your turning chains and continue.

METHOD 3: MAGIC RING (MR)

Also called a magic circle (mc). To begin, create a loop (as if to create a slipknot), hold the yarn where the loop crosses over, with the starting tail in front, and insert your hook from front to back.

• Yarn over with the working yarn and pull up a loop back through to the front. Yarn over your hook again, this time from above the loop, and pull through to create a chain on your ring.

• To create your first dc, insert your hook into the ring, with both the loop and starting tail above your hook. Your stitches will now be created around both yarns. Yarn over and draw up a loop back to the front of the ring. Create your stitch as you would usually. Carry on until you have the number of stitches you need.

• Once you have created all of your stitches, keep your hook in the loop and hold it and your round in your dominant hand. Pull on the starting tail to close the gap.

WORKING IN THE ROUND

CONTINUOUS SPIRAL

To start each new round, work the first stitch into the top of the first stitch of the last round. Now add your stitch marker into this stitch by slipping it through the loops. Now continue to stitch the rest of your round as stated in the pattern until you reach the stitch before the marker. This is the last stitch of the round.

To start your next round, remove the marker, crochet the stitch as normal and then replace the marker into the stitch you have just created.

When finishing your spiral you will need to smooth out the jump in stitches between rows. To do so, slip stitch into the next stitch. For taller stitches, gradually crochet shorter stitches i.e if you have used tr stitches you will end with a htr, dc, ss.

JOINED ROUNDS

Alternatively you can add a ss at the end of each row which gives the appearance of concentric circles rather than a spiral. If you do this, to create your next round, create a chain to the height of your stitch. One for double, two for half treble, three for treble and so on.

Turned

Not turned

TURN YOUR WORK

When you create your next rows you have the choice of turning your work or continuing on around the circle (the same as a spiral stitch). Alternatively, you can turn your work at the end of each round, and it will create a slightly different look. After turning your work, you will continue to work each of the rounds the same way.

FASTENING OFF

SECURE YOUR WORK

When you've finished your project, cut the working yarn about 15cm (6in) from the last stitch (or longer if your pattern states). Yarn over (yo) with the tail. Pull the yarn through the loop on your hook, and keep pulling until the cut end goes through the loop. Grab the tail and pull it tight, to close the last loop. Your stitches are now secure.

FIXING MISTAKES

UNDO YOUR WORK

When you notice that things have gone awry, take your hook out of the working loop and grab hold of the working yarn. Pull on the working yarn to unravel the stitches one by one. This process is also known as frogging. Keep pulling the working yarn until you've unravelled the mistake, then simply insert your hook into the working loop and begin redoing the work you've just undone, but this time without the mistake!

JOINING

METHOD 1: WHIP STITCH

Hold two pieces together with the wrong sides facing each other. Pass your needle through the V stitches on both pieces from front to back and pull the yarn through. Draw your needle back to the front and repeat. Using a whip stitch will leave a visible line on both sides of the piece. This won't be quite as obvious when you are using the same colour.

METHOD 2: MATTRESS STITCH

Lay your pieces side-by-side with the right sides facing you. Leaving a 15cm tail, insert your needle into the first edge stitch of the first piece and then down through the edge of the second. Insert your needle down through the first stitch of piece one and up through to the second stitch. Now repeat on piece two. Keep going and a loose 'ladder' will start to form. When you have done about 2.5cm, pull gently on the yarn to draw the two sides together. Repeat until you have reached the end, the seam will be almost invisible.

METHOD 3: SLIP STITCH OR DOUBLE CROCHET

Insert your hook through the first stitch on both pieces. Complete a slip stitch (or double crochet) and repeat, ensuring you match up the stitches as you go.

- A slip stitch seam is strong, and will be almost invisible from the other side of the work. Slip stitches do not allow for any give, so making them too tight will pucker the fabric.
- Using a double crochet will give a more pronounced edge, giving a more decorative seam. It is also stretchier than a slip stitch join.

METHOD 4: FLAT SLIP-STITCHED SEAM

Insert your hook from top to bottom through the back loop only on the right-hand piece of fabric. Do the same on your left piece, then yarn over (yo) and pull through both loops on the hook. Repeat until you reach the end. This seam produces a flat row of chain-looking stitches. It's a neat finish and adds a nice little detail to your seams.

To join amigurumi it is helpful to pin your pieces in place. Join using one of the methods above, inserting your needle from bottom to top of the piece you are attaching. Pull tight on the yarn for a seamless join.

YARN WEIGHTS

Yarn weight	Properties	Ideal for...
Lace, 2-ply, fingering	Extremely light, Lace yarn produces a very delicate texture on a 2mm (US 0) hook. Bigger hooks will produce a more open fabric.	Lace
Superfine, 3-ply, fingering, baby	Using a very slim hook, Superfine yarn is perfect for lightweight, intricate lace work.	Finely woven socks, shawls, babywear
Fine, 4-ply, sport, baby	Fine yarn is great for socks, and can also be used in items that feature slightly more delicate textures.	Light jumpers, babywear, socks, accessories
Double knit (DK), light worsted, 5/6-ply	An extremely versatile weight yarn, DK can be used to create a wide variety of items and crochets up relatively quickly.	Jumpers, light-weight scarves, blankets, toys
Aran, medium worsted, Afghan, 12-ply	With many yarns in this thickness using a variety of fibres to make them machine washable, Aran yarn is good for garments with thick cabled detail and functional items.	Jumpers, cabled garments, blankets, hats, scarves, mittens
Chunky, bulky, craft, rug, 14-ply	Quick to crochet, chunky yarn is perfect for warm outerwear. Often made from lightweight fibres to prevent drooping.	Rugs, jackets, blankets, hats, legwarmers, winter accessories
super chunky, super bulky, bulky, roving, 16-ply and upwards	Commonly used with very large hooks, Super chunky yarn crochets up very quickly. Large stitches make mistakes easy to spot.	Heavy blankets, rugs, thick scarves

HOOK SIZE CONVERSION TABLE

UK Size	US Size
2mm, 2.25mm	B/1
2.5mm, 2.75mm	C/2
3mm, 3.25mm	D/3
3.5mm	E/4
3.75mm, 4mm	F/5
4mm, 4.25mm	G/6
4.5mm	G/7
5mm	H/8
5.5mm	I/9
6mm	J/10
6.5mm, 7mm	K/10.5
8mm	L/11
9mm	M/13
10mm	N,P/15

TENSION

Tension or gauge is the measure of how many stitches and rows you need to create a specific length and width of crocheted fabric. The size of your hook, weight of your yarn and your own tension while crocheting will all have an effect on any piece that you're creating. If you naturally crochet very tight or loose stitches, then the final product dimensions will be different to those provided in a pattern. Tension square patterns will sometimes be given with your pattern and allow you to work out how tight to make your stitches before you start. Usually these will be 10cm square.

When making things like children's toys or blankets, there is a bit more freedom when following a pattern. However, when creating garments to exact fitted measurements, tension squares are incredibly important.

With amigurumi a loose tension will show the stuffing between the stitches. It's difficult to be too tight with amigurumi, however you should still be able to work stitches reasonably easily. If needed, switch to a smaller hook for a neater finish.

WHICH HOOK?

Every ball of yarn comes with a recommended hook size, which is printed on the label. Use bigger hooks than this to make a more open stitch, and smaller ones to make a tighter, more compact fabric. We suggest using a smaller hook than recommended for amigurumi projects.

AMIGURUMI TENSION TOO LOOSE

AMIGURUMI CORRECT TENSION

BLOCKING

Blocking is a process you will use after making many of your flat projects. It sets the stitches in place, adds definition to lace pieces and strengthens any straight edges in your work.

PIN YOUR WORK

No matter which method you choose to use, you will need to pin the corners to the correct measurement for your final piece.

Next pin half way along the edge, and keep doing this until you are happy that the edges are all straight and even. If you are blocking any crocheted segments that are due to be joined, make sure you measure them out so they match when you come to sew them together.

For more refined edging, thread a blocking wire through each of the stitches or row ends along the straight edge of your project.

METHOD 1: SPRAY BLOCKING

Spray blocking is the easiest and quickest way of blocking your work. Pin and then take a spray bottle and give a few sprays of water until the surface of your work is evenly saturated. Gently pat the surface to help the water absorb into the yarn fibres. Leave your work to dry; this can sometimes take over 24 hours.

METHOD 2: STEAM BLOCKING

This method requires an iron or handheld steamer. Do not touch the iron to the yarn at any point. Man-made fibres will melt, and all your work and your iron will be damaged. Pin your work then hold an iron about 2.5cm (1in) from the surface of your project. Steam until the entire surface area is moist to the touch. Once done, pat the surface gently with your hands and leave to dry.

METHOD 3: WET BLOCKING (BEST FOR LACE WORK)

Fill your sink or bath with lukewarm water. You can add in no-rinse wool wash if you wish. Immerse your project in the water, until saturated. Leave it for 20 minutes then take your project out and gently squeeze out the excess liquid. Do not wring your project, as this will stretch it out of shape. Continue until you can remove no more water. Lay a towel on a flat surface and lie your garment flat. Gently roll up your towel to press out even more water. Pin your project to your blocking surface (a foam mat or mattress is ideal) and leave to dry. If working on a straight-edged lace garment you will need to use a lot of pins and/or blocking wire along the edge of to obtain a professional result. The edge will bow if you don't use enough pins and spoil the finish.

ADDITIONAL USEFUL TERMS

ASTERISK* /BRACKETS [ ]
A symbol used to mark a point in a pattern row, usually at the beginning of a set of repeated instructions.

CHART/STITCH DIAGRAM
A visual depiction of a crochet pattern that uses symbols to represent stitches.

CROSSED STITCHES
Two or more tall stitches that are crossed, one in front of the other, to create an X shape.

FIBREFILL
Toy stuffing used to stuff amigurumi projects.

LINKED STITCH
A variation of any standard tall stitch that links the stitch to its neighbour partway up the post to eliminate the gaps between stitches and form a solid fabric.

POST
The vertical stem of a stitch.

POST STITCH
A stitch formed by crocheting around the post of the stitch in the row or round below, so the stitch sits in front of (or behind) the surface of the fabric.

RIGHT SIDE (RS)
The side of a crocheted piece that's visible when finished.

ROUND (RND)
A line of stitches worked around a circular crocheted piece.

ROW
A line of stitches worked across a flat crocheted piece.

SPACE (SP)
A gap formed between or beneath stitches, often seen in lace patterns.

STITCH MARKER
A small tool you can slide into a crochet stitch to mark a position. You can use a scrap of yarn or a hairgrip instead.

TAIL
A short length of unworked yarn left at the start or end of a piece.

V
The two loops at the top of each stitch that from a sideways V shape; standard crochet stitches are worked into both these loops.

WEAVE IN
A method used to secure and hide the yarn tails by stitching them through your crocheted stitches.

WORKING LOOP
The single loop that remains on your hook after completing a crochet stitch.

WRONG SIDE (WS)
The side of a crocheted piece that will be hidden; the inside or back.

YARN WEIGHT
The thickness of the yarn (not the weight of a ball of yarn).

ABBREVIATIONS AND SYMBOLS

UK stitch name	Abbreviation	Symbol	Description
back loop	BL		The loop furthest from you at the top of the stitch.
back post double crochet	BPdc		Yarn over, insert the hook from the back to the front, then to the back around the post of the next stitch, yarn over and draw up a loop, (yarn over and draw through two loops) twice.
chain(s)	ch(s)		Yarn over and draw through the loop on the hook.
chain space(s)	ch-sp(s)		The space beneath one or more chains.
double crochet	dc	or	Insert the hook into the next stitch and draw up a loop, yarn over and draw through both loops on the hook.
double crochet 2 together	dc2tog		(Insert the hook into the next stitch and draw up a loop) twice, yarn over and draw through all three loops on the hook.
double treble crochet	dtr		Yarn over twice, insert the hook into the next stitch and draw up a loop, (yarn over and draw through two loops on the hook) three times.
front loop	FL		The loop closest to you at the top of the stitch.
front post treble crochet	FPtr		Yarn over, insert the hook from the front to the back to the front around the post of the next stitch, yarn over and draw up a loop, (yarn over and draw through two loops) twice.
half treble crochet	htr		Yarn over, insert the hook into the next stitch and draw up a loop, yarn over and draw through all three loops on the hook.
repeat	rep		Replicate a series of given instructions.
skip	sk		Pass over a stitch or stitches - do not work into it.
slip stitch	ss/sl st	or	Insert the hook into the next stitch, draw up a loop through the stitch and the loop on the hook.
stitch(es)	st(s)		A group of one or more loops of yarn pulled through each other in a specified order until only 1 remains on the hook.
treble crochet	tr		Yarn over, insert the hook into the next stitch and draw up a loop, (yarn over and draw through two loops on the hook) twice.
treble crochet 2 together	tr2tog		(Yarn over, insert the hook into the next stitch and draw up a loop, yarn over and draw through two loops on the hook) twice, yarn over and draw through all three loops on the hook.
turning chain	t-ch		The chain made at the start of a row to bring your hook and yarn up to the height of the next row.
yarn over	yo		Pass the yarn over the hook so the yarn is caught in the throat of the hook.

If a pattern requires stitches that are not mentioned in this essentials section, stitch instructions will be given on the pattern page.

Crochet GLOSSARY

AMIGURUMI
The Japanese art of knitting or crocheting small, stuffed yarn creatures.

ASTERISK*
A symbol used to mark a point in a pattern row, usually at the beginning of a set of repeated instructions.

BACK LOOP (BL) ONLY
A method of crocheting in which you work into only the back loop of a stitch instead of both loops.

BACK POST (BP) STITCHES
Textured stitches worked from the back around the post of the stitch below.

BALL BAND
The paper wrapper around a ball of yarn that contains information such as fibre content, amount/ length of yarn, weight, colour and dye lot.

BLOCK
A finishing technique that uses moisture to set stitches and shape pieces to their final measurements.

BLOCKING WIRE
A long, straight wire used to hold the edges of crochet pieces straight during blocking, most often for lace.

BOBBLE
A crochet stitch that stands out from the fabric, formed from several incomplete tall stitches joined at the top and bottom.

BRACKETS [ ]
Symbols used to surround a set of grouped instructions, often used to indicate repeats.

CHAIN (CH)
The most simple crochet stitch that often forms the foundation that other stitches are worked into.

CHAIN SPACE (CH-SP)
A gap formed beneath one or more chain stitches, usually worked into instead of into the individual chain(s).

CHAINLESS FOUNDATION
A stretchy foundation plus first row of stitches that are made in one step. Often used in flatwork pieces.

CHAINLESS FOUNDATION STITCHES
Stitches that have an extra chain at the bottom so they can be worked into without first crocheting a foundation chain.

CHART
A visual depiction of a crochet pattern that uses symbols to represent stitches.

CLUSTER
A combination stitch formed from several incomplete tall stitches joined at the top.

CONTRAST COLOUR (CC)
A yarn colour used as an accent to the project's main colour.

CROCHET HOOK
The tool used to form all crochet stitches.

CROSSED STITCHES
Two or more tall stitches that are crossed, one in front of the other, to create an X shape.

DECREASE (DEC)
A shaping technique in which you reduce the number of stitches in your work.

DOUBLE CROCHET
The most basic crochet stitch.

DOUBLE TREBLE CROCHET (DTR)
A basic crochet stitch three times as tall as a double crochet stitch.

DRAPE
The way in which your crocheted fabric hangs; how stiff or flowing it feels.

DRAW UP A LOOP
To pull up a loop of yarn through a stitch or space after inserting your hook into that stitch or space.

FAN
A group of several tall stitches crocheted into the same base stitch and usually separated by chains to form a fan shape.

FASTEN OFF
To lock the final stitch with the yarn end so the crocheted work cannot unravel.

FASTEN ON
To draw up a loop of new yarn through a stitch in preparation to begin crocheting.

FOUNDATION CHAIN
A base chain into which most crochet is worked (unless worked in the round).

FOUNDATION STITCHES, CHAINLESS
See chainless foundation stitches.

Did you know?
James Buchanan, US president between 1857 and 1861, liked to crochet in his free time.

knife grip

FRINGE
A decorative edging made from strands of yarn knotted along the edge.

FROG
To unravel your crochet work by removing your hook and pulling the working yarn. Not the animal.

FRONT LOOP (FL) ONLY
A method in which you work into only the front loop of a stitch instead of both loops.

FRONT POST (FP) STITCHES
Textured stitches worked from the front around the post of the stitch below.

GAUGE (TENSION)
See tension.

HALF TREBLE CROCHET
A basic stitch halfway between the height of a double and treble crochet stitch.

INCREASE (INC)
A shaping technique in which you add extra stitches to your work.

INVISIBLE FINISH
A method of finishing a round or edging so the join is not visible. This requires a yarn needle to finish.

KNIFE GRIP
An overhand method of holding a crochet hook, similar to holding a knife.

LINKED STITCH
A variation of any standard tall stitch that links the stitch to its neighbour partway up the post to eliminate the gaps between stitches and form a solid fabric.

LOOP STITCH
A stitch that creates a loop instead of pulling the stitch through completely.

MAGIC RING
A technique to begin working in the round without leaving a hole in the centre by crocheting over an adjustable loop.

MAIN COLOUR (MC)
The predominant yarn colour of a project.

MATTRESS STITCH
A stitch to sew a seam that forms an almost invisible join on the right side of the work and a ridged seam on the wrong side.

MOTIF
A crocheted shape usually worked in the round as a geometric shape and combined with other motifs into larger pieces.

PARENTHESES ()
Symbols used in crochet patterns to surround a set of grouped instructions, often used to indicate repeats.

PENCIL GRIP
An underhand method of holding a crochet hook, similar to holding a pencil.

PICOT
A tiny loop of chain stitches that sits on top of a stitch and creates a small shape.

POPCORN
A combination stitch that stands out from the fabric formed from several tall stitches pulled together by a chain stitch.

POST
The main vertical stem of a stitch.

POST STITCH
A stitch formed by crocheting around the post of the stitch in the row or round below, so the stitch sits in front of (or behind) the surface of the fabric.

PUFF STITCH
A combination crochet stitch that forms a smooth, puffy shape created from several incomplete half treble crochet stitches that are joined at the top and bottom.

REPEAT (REP)
To replicate a series of crochet instructions; one instance of the duplicated instructions.

REVERSE DOUBLE CROCHET
A variation of double crochet that is worked backwards (left to right) around the edge of a piece, producing a corded edging.

RIGHT SIDE (RS)
The side of a crocheted piece that's visible.

RIP BACK
To unravel your crochet work.

ROUND (RND)
A line of stitches worked around a circular crocheted piece.

ROW
A line of stitches worked across a flat crocheted piece.

SHELL
A group of several tall stitches, crocheted into the same base stitch, that spread out at the top into a shell shape.

SKIP (SK)
To pass over a stitch or stitches.

SLIP KNOT
A knot that can be tightened by pulling one end of the yarn; used for attaching the yarn to the hook to begin crocheting.

SLIP STITCH (SS OR SL ST)
A stitch with no height, primarily used to join rounds and stitches to move the hook and yarn into a new position.

SPACE (SP)
A gap formed between or beneath stitches, often seen in lace patterns.

SPIKE STICH
A stitch worked around existing stitches to extend down to one or more rows below, creating a long vertical spike.

STITCH (ST)
A group of one or more loops of yarn pulled through each other in a specific order until only one loop remains on the crochet hook.

STITCH DIAGRAM
A map of a crochet or stitch pattern, where each stitch is represented by a symbol.

STITCH MARKER
A small tool you can slide into a crochet stitch or between stitches to mark a position.

SWATCH
A crocheted sample of a stitch pattern large enough to measure the tension (gauge) and test the pattern with a specific hook and yarn.

TAIL
A short length of unworked yarn left at the start or end of a piece.

TENSION (GAUGE)
A measure of how many stitches and rows fit into a certain length of crocheted fabric, usually 10 centimetres (4 inches), that indicates the size of each stitch.

TOGETHER (TOG)
A shaping technique in which you work two or more stitches into one to reduce the number of stitches.

TREBLE CROCHET (TR)
A basic stitch twice as tall as a double crochet.

TURNING CHAIN (T-CH)
A chain made at the start of a row to bring your hook and yarn up to the height of the next row.

V
The two loops at the top of each stitch that form a sideways V shape; standard crochet stitches are worked into both these loops.

V STITCH
A group of two tall stitches crocheted into the same base stitch and separated by one or more chains, forming a V shape.

WEAVE IN
A method used to secure and hide the yarn tails by stitching them through your crocheted stitches.

WHIP STITCH
A simple stitch to sew a seam by inserting the needle through the edge of both crocheted pieces at once to form each stitch.

WORKING IN THE ROUND
Crocheting in a circle instead of back and forward in straight rows, particularly used in amigurumi projects.

WORKING LOOP
The single loop that remains on your hook after completing a crochet stitch.

WRONG SIDE (WS)
The side of a crocheted piece that will be hidden; the inside or back.

YARDAGE
A length of yarn, usually expressed as an estimate of the amount of yarn required for a project.

YARN NEEDLE
A wide, blunt-tipped needle with an eye large enough for the yarn to pass through that's used for stitching crocheted pieces together and weaving in ends.

YARN OVER (YO)
To pass the yarn over the hook so the yarn is caught in the throat of the hook in order to create longer stitches.

YARN TAIL
See tail.

YARN WEIGHT
The thickness of the yarn (not the literal weight of a ball or yarn).

Baby

26
Rainbow rattle

30
Lamb lovey

34
Hushabye sleeping bag

38
Koala teether and rattle

42
Hot air balloon mobile

46
Sherbet stripes blanket

Rainbow rattle

Your little one is sure to love this colorful rattle, and you'll love how quick and easy it is to make

DESIGNED BY

JENNI CATAVU

Designer info: Jenni is a crochet designer from the US, where she lives with her family and is inspired by her four sons to keep creating! Find Jenni's free patterns online.
www.byjennidesigns.com
@byjennidesigns

DIFFICULTY

WHAT YOU NEED

- 3.75mm hook (US F/5)
- Yarn needle
- Fibrefill stuffing
- Disc rattle insert, no larger than 20mm diameter x 10mm thickness
- Aran (worsted weight) yarn in small amounts. Here we have used:

Colour 1: Violet
Colour 2: Indigo/Navy
Colour 3: Blue
Colour 4: Green
Colour 5: Yellow
Colour 6: Orange
Colour 7: Red
Colour 8: White

MEASUREMENTS

14 x 7cm (5½ x 2¾in)

TENSION

23 stitches and 22 rows to measure 10 x 10cm (4 x 4in) over dc, using 3.75mm hook

PATTERN

RAINBOW

Using col 1, ch 17.

Row 1: Starting in the 2nd ch from hook, dc2tog, 1 dc in next 12 sts, dc2tog. Fasten off & turn. (14 sts)

Row 2: Using col 2, join in first st, ch 1, 2 dc in first st, 1 dc in next 12 sts, 2 dc in last st. Fasten off & turn. (16 sts)

Row 3: Using col 3, join in first st, ch 1, 2 dc in first st, 1 dc in next 5 sts, 2 dc in next st, 1 dc in next 2 sts, 2 dc in next st, 1 dc in next 5 sts, 2 dc in last st. Fasten off & turn. (20 sts)

Row 4: Using col 4, join in first st, ch 1, 2 dc in first st, 1 dc in next 18 sts, 2 dc in last st. Fasten off & turn. (22 sts)

Row 5: Using col 5, join in first st, ch 1, 2 dc in first st, 1 dc in next 4 sts, 2 dc in next st, 1 dc in next 4 sts, 2 dc in next 2 sts, 1 dc in next 4 sts, 2 dc in next st, 1 dc in next 4 sts, 2 dc in last st. Fasten off & turn. (28 sts)

Row 6: Using col 6, join in first st, ch 1, 2 dc in first st, 1 dc in next 26 sts, 2 dc in last st. Fasten off & turn. (30 sts)

Row 7: Using col 7, join in first st, ch 1, 1 htr in first st, 1 dc in next 28 sts, 1 htr in last st. Fasten off & turn. (30 sts)

Row 8: Using col 6, join in first st, ch 1, 1 dc in each st. Fasten off & turn. (30 sts)

Row 9: Using col 5, join in first st, ch 1, dc2tog, 1 dc in next 26 sts, dc2tog. Fasten off & turn. (28 sts)

Row 10: Using col 4, join in first st, ch 1, dc2tog, 1 dc in next 4 sts, dc2tog, 1 dc in next 4 sts, dc2tog, dc2tog, 1 dc in next 4 sts, dc2tog, 1 dc in next 4 sts, dc2tog, Fasten off & turn. (22 sts)

Row 11: Using col 3, join in first st, ch 1, dc2tog, 1 dc in next 18 sts, dc2tog. Fasten off & turn. (20 sts)

Row 12: Using col 2, join in first st, ch 1, dc2tog, 1 dc in next 5 sts, dc2tog, 1 dc in next 2 sts, dc2tog, 1 dc in next 5 sts, dc2tog. (16 sts)

The side currently facing you is the right side. Fasten off leaving a long end to sew the rainbow shut.

Turn the piece over so the wrong side is facing you and sew in the ends, except for the last end indicated to leave long. For a tidy clean look it's important to sew the ends in on the wrong side.

Using the long end (with the wrong side still facing you), fold the piece in half so that you can sew the edge of row 1 to the edge of row 12. After you have the rainbow sewn shut you can sew in this end.

Stuff the rainbow and set aside.

CLOUDS

CENTER PIECE (MAKE 2)

Using col 8, make a magic ring.

Row 1: Ch 1, work 6 dc into the ring, ss in beginning ch 1 to join. (6 sts)

Row 2: Ch 1, 2 dc in each st, ss in ch 1 to join. (12 sts)

Row 3: Ch 1, (2 dc in next st, 1 dc in next st) 6 times, ss in ch 1 to join. (18 sts)

Row 4: Ch 1, (2 dc in next st, 1 dc in next 5 sts) 3 times, ss in ch 1 to join. (21 sts)

Row 5: Ch 1, 1 dc in each st, ss in ch 1 to join. (21 sts)

Row 6: Ch 1, (dc in next 5 sts, dc2tog) 3 times, ss in ch 1 to join. (18 sts)

Row 7: Ch 1, (1 dc in next st, dc2tog) 6 times, ss in ch 1 to join. (12 sts)

Pull your beginning magic ring tight and sew in the end. Begin to stuff with fibrefill, and if you are using a rattle insert it should be added at this time.

"The vibrant rainbow colours will be sure to grab the attention of your baby"

Row 8: Ch 1, (dc2tog) 6 times, ss in ch 1 to join. Fasten off leaving a long end for sewing. (6 sts)

Finish stuffing with fibrefill and use the long end to sew hole shut. Set piece aside and continue on to the side pieces.

SIDE PIECE (MAKE 4)

Using col 8, make a magic ring.

Row 1: Ch 1, work 6 dc into the ring, ss in beginning ch 1 to join. (6 sts)

Row 2: Ch 1, 2 dc in each st, ss in ch 1 to join. (12 sts)

Row 3: Ch 1, 1 dc in each st, ss in ch 1 to join. (12 sts)

Row 4: Ch 1, dc2tog, 1 dc in next 4 sts, dc2tog, 1 dc in next 4 sts, ss in ch 1 to join. Fasten off leaving a long end for sewing. (10 sts)

Stuff with fibrefill.

Assemble cloud by sewing 1 side piece to each side of the centre piece.

Use col 8 to sew a cloud to each end of the rainbow.

Sewing a cloud to each end of the rainbow adds interest and completes the rattle

Lamb lovey

Create this cute and cuddly security blanket, the perfect gift for any baby

DIFFICULTY

✂ ✂ ✂ ✂ ✂

WHAT YOU NEED

- 4.5mm hook (US 7)
- Yarn needle
- Fibrefill stuffing
- A pair of 10mm black safety eyes
- You will need to use DK yarn in your chosen colour. Here we have used Deramores Studio DK in:

Colour 1: White (3 balls)

Colour 2: Grey (1 ball)

MEASUREMENTS

55cm (21¾in) diameter

TENSION

16 sts x 16 rows to measure 10x10cm (4x4in), over pattern using 4.5mm hook

SPECIAL STITCHES:

Bobble Stitch (bo): *Yoh, insert hook into stitch or space indicated, yoh and pull a loop through so you now have 3 loops on your hook. Yoh and pull through 2 loops. Repeat this step from *, 4 more times in the same stitch or space, until you have 6 loops on your hook. Yoh and pull through all 6 loops.

Modified Bobble Stitch (mbo): This is almost identical to the regular bobble stitch (bo), but it uses 4 unfinished tr stitches clustered together in the same stitch instead of the regular 5 (therefore having 5 loops on your hook before the final yoh).

Three Treble Crochet Cluster (tr3cl): 3 tr stitches in the same stitch/space.

Corner 1: (1 tr, ch 2, 1 tr) in the same stitch (for round 3) or chain space (for rest of rounds).

Corner 2: (2 dc, ch 2, 2 dc) in the same chain space.

Dec: work a dc2tog as follows: insert hook in first st, yoh and pull a loop through, insert hook in next st, yoh and pull a loop through, yoh and pull through all 3 loops.

PATTERN

STAR-SHAPED LOVEY

Using col 1, make a magic ring.

Rnd 1 (RS): Work 10 dc into the ring. (10 sts)

Rnd 2: ([1 dc and 1 tr3cl] in next st) 10 times, ss into 1st st. (20 sts)

Rnd 3: (1 dc in next st, Corner 1 in next st, 1 dc in next st, sk next st) 5 times, ss into 1st st. (30 sts)

Rnd 4: (1 dc in next st, Corner 2 in next st, 1 dc in next st, dec) 5 times. (45 sts)

Rnd 5: (1 dc in next st, mbo in next st, 1 dc in next st, Corner 1 in next st, 1 dc in next st, mbo in next st, 1 dc in next st, sk next st) 5 times, ss into 1st st. (50 sts)

Rnd 6: (1 dc in next 3 sts, Corner 2 in next st, 1 dc in next 3 sts, dec) 5 times. (65 sts)

Rnd 7: ([1 dc in next st, mbo in next st] twice, 1 dc in next st, Corner 1 in next st, 1 dc in next st, [mbo in next st, 1 dc in next st] twice, sk 1 st) 5 times, ss in 1st st. (70 sts)

Rnd 8: (1 dc in next 5 sts, Corner 2 in next st, 1 dc in next 5 sts, dec) 5 times. (85 sts)

Rnd 9: ([1 dc in next st, mbo in next st] 3 times, 1 dc in next st, Corner 1 in next st, 1 dc in next st, [mbo in next st, 1 dc in next st] 3 times, sk 1 st) 5 times, ss into 1st st. (90 sts)

Rnd 10: (1 dc into next 7 sts, Corner 2 in next st, 1 dc in next 7 sts, dec) 5 times. (105 sts)

Rnd 11: ([1 dc in next st, mbo in next st] 4 times, 1 dc in next st, Corner 1 in next st, 1 dc in next st, [mbo in next st, 1 dc in next st] 4 times, sk 1 st) 5 times, ss into 1st st. (110 sts)

Rnd 12: (1 dc in next 9 sts, Corner 2 in next st, 1 dc in next 9 sts, dec) 5 times. (125 sts)

Rnd 13: ([1 dc in next st, mbo in next st] 5 times, 1 dc in next st, Corner 1 in next st, 1 dc in next st, [mbo in next st, 1 dc in next st] 5 times, sk 1 st) 5 times, ss into 1st st. (130 sts)

Rnd 14: (1 dc in next 11 sts, Corner 2 in next st, 1 dc in next 11 sts, dec) 5 times. (145 sts)

Rnd 15: ([1 dc in next st, mbo in next st] 6 times, 1 dc in next st, Corner 1 in next st, 1 dc in next st, [mbo in next st, 1 dc in next st] 6 times, sk 1 st) 5 times, ss into 1st st. (150 sts)

Rnd 16: (1 dc in next 13 sts, Corner 2 in next st, 1 dc in next 13 sts, dec) 5 times. (165 sts)

Rnd 17: ([1 dc in next st, mbo in next st] 7 times, 1 dc in next st, Corner 1 in next st, 1 dc in next st, [mbo in next st, 1 dc in next st] 7 times, sk 1 st) 5 times, ss into 1st st. (170 sts)

Rnd 18: (1 dc in next 15 sts, Corner 2 in next st, 1 dc in next 15 sts, dec) 5 times. (185 sts)

Rnd 19: ([1 dc in next st, mbo in next st] 8 times, 1 dc in next st, Corner 1 in next st, 1 dc in next st, [mbo in next st, 1 dc in next st] 8 times, sk 1 st) 5 times, ss into 1st st. (190 sts)

Rnd 20: (1 dc in next 17 sts, Corner 2 in next st, 1 dc in next 17 sts,

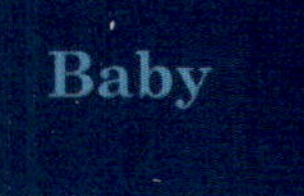

PATTERN NOTES

- In each round, the corner chains are included in the stitch count.
- You only join the round on rnd 2 and following alternate rounds.

DESIGNED BY

ARIANA WIMSETT

Ariana is the crochet designer behind Crafting Happiness. She specialises in nursery decor, blankets and amigurumi toys, and her patterns are fun and easy to make, designed with the beginner crocheter in mind. ***https://craftinghappiness.com/ https://www.facebook.com/CraftingHappinessCrochet/ Ravelry: https://www.ravelry.com/designers/crafting-happiness***

dec) 5 times. (205 sts)
Rnd 21: ([1 dc in next st, mbo in next st] 9 times, 1 dc in next st, Corner 1 in next st, 1 dc in next st, [mbo in next st, 1 dc in next st] 9 times, sk 1 st) 5 times, ss into next st. (210 sts)
Rnd 22: (1 dc in next 19 sts, Corner 2 in next st, 1 dc in next 19 sts, dec) 5 times. (225 sts)
Rnd 23: ([1 dc in next st, mbo in next st] 10 times, 1 dc in next st, Corner 1 in next st, 1 dc in next st, [mbo in next st, 1 dc in next st] 10 times, sk 1 st) 5 times, ss into 1st st. (230 sts)
Rnd 24: (1 dc in next 21 sts, Corner 2 in next st, 1 dc in next 21 sts, dec) 5 times. (245 sts)
Rnd 25: ([1 dc in next st, mbo in next st] 11 times, 1 dc in next st, Corner 1 in next st, 1 dc in next st, [mbo in next st, 1 dc in next st] 11 times, sk 1 st) 5 times, ss into 1st st. (250 sts)
Rnd 26: (1 dc in next 23 sts, Corner 2 in next st, 1 dc in next 23 sts, dec) 5 times. (265 sts)
Rnd 27: ([1 dc in next st, mbo in next st] 12 times, 1 dc in next st, Corner 1 in next st, 1 dc in next st, [mbo in next st, 1 dc in next st] 12 times, sk 1 st) 5 times, ss into 1st st. (270 sts)
Rnd 28: (1 dc in next 25 sts, Corner 2 in next st, 1 dc in next 25 sts, dec) 5 times. (285 sts)
Rnd 29: ([1 dc in next st, mbo in next st] 13 times, 1 dc in next st, Corner 1 in next st, 1 dc in next st, [mbo in next st, 1 dc in next st] 13 times, sk 1 st) 5 times, ss into 1st st. (290 sts)

Change to col 2.

Rnd 30: (1 dc in next 27 sts, Corner 2 in next st, 1 dc in next 27 sts, dec) 5 times. (305 sts)
Rnd 31: (1 dc in next 29 sts, Corner 2 in next st, 1 dc in next 29 sts, sk 1 st) 5 times. (320 sts)

Finish off and weave in ends.

HEAD

Using col 2, make a magic ring.
Rnd 1 (RS): Work 6 dc into the ring. (6 sts)
Rnd 2: 2 dc in each st. (12 sts)
Rnd 3: (2 dc in next st, 1 dc in next st) 6 times. (18 sts)
Rnd 4: (2 dc in next st, 1 dc in next 2 sts) 6 times. (24 sts)
Rnds 5-6: 1 dc in each st. (24 sts)
Rnd 7: (2 dc in next st, 1 dc in next 3 sts) 6 times. (30 sts)
Rnds 8-9: 1 dc in each st. (30 sts)
Rnd 10: (2 dc in next st, 1 dc in next 4 sts) 6 times. (36 sts)
Rnds 11-12: 1 dc in each st. (36 sts)

Change to col 1.

Rnd 13: 1 dc in each st. (36 sts)
Rnd 14: (1 dc in next st, 1 bo in next st) to end. (36 sts)
Rnd 15: (2 dc in next st, 1 dc in next 3 sts) 9 times. (45 sts)
Rnd 16: (1 dc in next st, 1 bo in next st) to last st, 1 dc in last st. (45 sts)
Rnd 17: 1 dc in each st. (45 sts)
Rnd 18: 1 bo in next st, (1 dc in next st, 1 bo in next st) to end. (45 sts)
Rnd 19: 1 dc in each st. (45 sts)
Rnd 20: 1 bo in next st, (1 dc in next st, 1 bo in next st) to end. (45 sts)
Rnd 21: (Dec, 1 dc in next 3 sts) 9 times. (36 sts)

Place the eyes 10 stitches apart, between rnds 10 and 11. Start filling the head with fibrefill and continue stuffing as you work.

Rnd 22: (1 dc in next st, 1 bo in next st) to end. (36 sts)
Rnd 23: (Dec, 1 dc in next 2 sts) 9 times. (27 sts)
Rnd 24: 1 bo in next st, (1 dc in next st, 1 bo in next st) to end. (27 sts)
Rnd 25: (Dec, 1 dc in next st) 9 times. (18 sts)

A blanket and teddy all in one

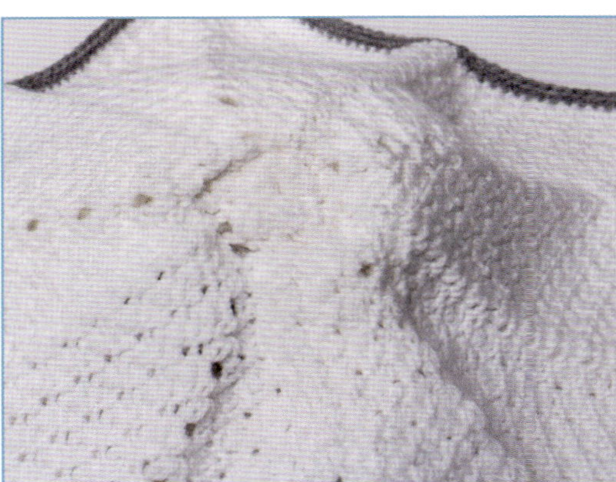

Rnd 26: (1 dc in next st, 1 bo in next st) to end. (18 sts)
Rnd 27: (Dec, 1 dc in next st) 6 times. (12 sts)
Rnd 28: (1 dc in next st, 1 bo in next st) 6 times. (12 sts)

Fasten off and finish filling up the head. Cut the yarn leaving a long tail, and use it to close up the hole in the head.

EARS (MAKE 2)

Using col 2, make a magic ring.
Rnd 1: Work 6 dc into the ring. (6 sts)
Rnd 2: 2 dc in each st. (12 sts)
Rnd 3: (2 dc in next st, 1 dc in next st) 6 times. (18 sts)
Rnds 4-8: 1 dc in each st. (18 sts)
Rnd 9: (Dec, 1 dc in next st) 6 times. (12 sts)
Rnds 10-12: 1 dc in each st. (12 sts)

Flatten ear and ss through both layers. Finish off, leaving a long tail for sewing.

LEGS (MAKE 2)

Using col 2, make a magic ring.
Rnd 1: Work 6 dc into the ring. (6 sts)
Rnd 2: 2 dc in each st. (12 sts)
Rnd 3: (2 dc in next st, 1 dc in next st) 6 times. (18 sts)
Rnd 4: (2 dc in next st, 1 dc in next 5 sts) 3 times. (21 sts)
Rnds 5-9: 1 dc in each st. (21 sts)

Change to col 1.

Rnd 10: 1 dc in each st. (21 sts)
Rnd 11: 1 dc in next 19 sts, dec. (20 sts)
Rnd 12: 1 dc in each st. (20 sts)
Rnd 13: 1 dc in next 9 sts, dec, 1 dc in next 9 sts. (19 sts)
Rnd 14: 1 dc in each st. (19 sts)
Rnd 15: 1 dc in next 17 sts, dec. (18 sts)
Rnd 16: 1 dc in each st. (18 sts)

Start stuffing the leg with fibrefill. Continue stuffing as you work.

Rnd 17: 1 dc in next 8 sts, dec, 1 dc in next 8 sts. (17 sts)
Rnd 18: 1 dc in each st. (17 sts)
Rnd 19: 1 dc in next 15 sts, dec. (16 sts)
Rnd 20: 1 dc in each st. (16 sts)
Rnd 21: 1 dc in next 7 sts, dec, 1 dc in next 7 sts. (15 sts)
Rnd 22: 1 dc in each st. (15 sts)
Rnd 23: 1 dc in next 13 sts, dec. (14 st)
Rnd 25: 1 dc in each st. (14 sts)

Finish filling leg, flatten edge and ss through both layers. Finish off, leaving a long tail for sewing.

ASSEMBLY

Fold each ear in half and sew a couple of stitches through the base, then sew them onto the head.

Hushabye sleeping bag

Reminiscent of 'granny' squares, this simple sleeping bag is perfect for newborn babies to snuggle up in

DIFFICULTY

✂ ✂ ✂ ✂ ✂

WHAT YOU NEED

- 4mm hook (US G/6)
- 10 x 2.5cm (1 in) buttons
- You will need DK weight yarn in your chosen colours. We have used Sublime baby Cashmere Merino Silk DK in: safety eyes

Colour 1: Pebble (250g)
Colour 2: Vanilla (100g)
Colour 3: Splash (50g)

TENSION

Tension is not critical for this project, but if you do not match it your sleeping bag will vary in size to that stated and you may need more yarn. 5 pattern repeats and 11 rows measure 10cm square, using 4mm hook

MEASUREMENTS

Sleeping Bag measures 37cm wide and 44cm long excluding hood. Hood measures approx 23cm from top of bag to point

SPECIAL STITCHES

Crab stitch/reverse dc: Yo and draw up a loop, making sure your hook faces left as it would usually. Complete the stitch as normal and then continue to work backwards along your edge. Make sure not to twist your hook!

PATTERN

FRONT

Using 4mm hook and col 1, ch 55.

Row 1 (RS): 3 tr in 7th ch from hook, *miss 2 ch, 3 tr in next ch; rep from * to last 3 ch, miss 2 ch, tr in last st, turn. Place a marker at the end of this row to mark fold line. (16 treble clusters and 2 edge sts)

Row 2: ch 3 (counts as 1st tr), 1 tr in ch-sp before next treble cluster, *3 tr in each space between treble clusters along the row to last ch-sp, 2 tr in last ch-sp, turn. (15 treble clusters with 2 half clusters)

Row 3: ch 3 (counts as 1st tr), 3 tr in each space between treble clusters along the row to last 2 tr, skip next tr, 1 tr in top of beginning ch 3 of previous row. (16 treble clusters and 2 edge sts)

Rows 2 and 3 form pattern. Cont working in pattern for remainder of piece, working in stripes as follows:

Rows 4-5: 2 rows with col 1.
Row 6: 1 row with col 2.
Rows 7-8: 2 rows with col 1.
Rows 9-11: 3 rows with col 3.
Rows 12-13: 2 rows with col 1.
Row 14: 1 row with col 2.
Rows 15-19: 5 rows with col 1.
Row 20: 1 row with col 3.
Rows 21-22: 2 rows with col 1.
Rows 23-25: 3 rows with col 2.
Rows 26-27: 2 rows with col 1.
Row 28: 1 row with col 3.
Rows 29-33: 5 rows with col 1.
Row 34: 1 row with col 2.
Rows 35-36: 2 rows with col 1.
Rows 37-39: 3 rows with col 3.
Rows 40-41: 2 rows with col 1.
Row 42: 1 row with col 2.
Rows 43-44: 2 rows with col 1.
Fasten off.

BACK AND HOOD

Using col 1 and with RS facing, rotate work and fasten on at the marker to begin working along bottom of piece (this will be the fold line along the bottom of the bag). Continue working in pattern throughout in stripes as follows:

Rows 1-5: 5 rows with col 1.
Row 6: 1 row with col 2.
Rows 7-8: 2 rows with col 1.
Rows 9-11: 3 rows with col 3.
Rows 12-13: 2 rows with col 1.
Row 14: 1 row with col 2.
Rows 15-19: 5 rows with col 1.

DESIGNED BY

DONNA JONES

Donna designs, edits and teaches yarn crafts. She believes creative expression is essential for our wellbeing and aims to instil this in others.

Follow her on Instagram *@djonesdesigns*
www.donnajonesdesigns.co.uk

PATTERN NOTES

• This project is sized for a newborn baby. It is simple to adjust the size to suit larger babies as well. To adjust the width add sts to the foundation chain in multiples of 3; to adjust length add rows. Don't forget you will need more yarn to make a bigger sleeping bag.

• For baby's safety it is important to ensure the bag is not so large they can slip down too far as this can cause them to get overheated. As with any bedding, their face should remain above the cover, which should tuck under their arms, and make sure they are placed with their feet at the end of their crib, Moses basket, pram etc.

Row 20: 1 row with col 3.
Rows 21-22: 2 rows with col 1.
Rows 23-25: 3 rows with col 2.
Rows 26-27: 2 rows with col 1.
Row 28: 1 row with col 3.
Rows 29-33: 5 rows with col 1.
Row 34: 1 row with col 2.
Rows 35-36: 2 rows with col 1.
Rows 37-39: 3 rows with col 3.
Rows 40-41: 2 rows with col 1.
Row 42: 1 row with col 2.
Rows 43-47: 5 rows with col 1.
Rows 48: 1 row with col 2. Place marker at each end of this row.
Rows 49-50: 2 rows with col 1.
Rows 50-53: 3 rows with col 3.
Rows 54-55: 2 rows with col 1.
Row 56: 1 row with col 2.
Rows 57-61: 5 rows with col 1.
Row 62: 1 row with col 3.
Rows 63-64: 2 rows with col 1.
Rows 65-67: 3 rows with col 2.
Rows 68-69: 2 rows with col 1.
Row 70: 1 row with col 3.
Rows 71-74: 4 rows with col 1.
Do not fasten off.

FORM AND SEAM HOOD

Fold the top edge of the work in half with RS facing together, join together along top edge with dc to form hood.
Fasten off.
Sew in all ends to WS of work

EDGING

With RS facing and using col 1, fasten on at the marker on the fold line. Begin working in rounds as follows:
Rnd 1: ch 1, (placing marker or safety pin in first st) work 2 dc in each row edge of tr down left side edge, across hood, up along edge to corner, 3 dc in the corner st, 1 dc in each st along front top edge, 3 dc in the corner st, 2 dc in each row wof tr up right side edge, and ss to first (marked) dc.
Remove marker.
Rnds 2-5: ch 1, 1 dc same place (replacing marker or safety pin in first st), 1 dc in each dc around edge, working 3 dc in each corner, join with ss in first (marked) dc.
Remove marker.
With RS facing, and front positioned over back ensuring edge of front lines up with markers placed at each end of Row 48 of back, place 5 markers evenly along the two front side edges to indicate placement of buttonholes.
Rnd 6 (Buttonholes): ch 1, 1 dc in same place (placing marker or safety pin in first st), 1 dc in each dc to 1 st before first marker, (3ch, skip 3 dc, 1 dc in each dc to 1 st before next marker) 4 times, 3ch, skip 3 dc, 1 dc in each dc to top corner of front, 3 dc in the corner st, 1 dc in each dc along front top edge, 3 dc in the corner st, (1 dc in each dc to 1 st before next marker, 3ch, skip 3 dc) 5 times, 1 dc in each dc to end, join with a ss in first (marked) dc. Remove all markers.
Rnd 7: ch 1, 1 dc in same place (replacing marker or safety pin in first st), 1 dc in each dc to first 3 ch-sp, (3 dc in 3 ch-sp, 1 dc in each dc to next 3 ch-sp) 4 times, 3 dc in next 3ch-sp, 1 dc in each dc to top corner of front, 3 dc in the corner st, 1 dc in each dc along front top edge, 3 dc in the corner st, (1 dc in each dc to next 3 ch-sp, 3 dc in ch-sp) 5 times, 1 dc in each dc to end, join with a ss in first (marked) dc.
Remove marker.
Rnds 8-10: ch 1, 1 dc in same place (placing marker or safety pin in first st), 1 dc in each dc along side edge of back, across hood, along second side edge of back to top corner of front, 3 dc in the corner st, 1 dc in each dc along front top edge, 3 dc in the corner st, 1 dc in each dc along side edge of front, join with a ss into first (marked) dc.
Remove marker

REVERSE DC EDGING

Change to col 2.
Next Rnd: ch 1, 1 rdc in each dc around edge, working 3 rev dc in each of the 2 corners, join with a ss to first rdc.
Fasten off.

FINISHING

Sew in all remaining ends and spray block. Sew buttons on back edging to correspond with buttonholes.

Koala teether and rattle

The perfect gift for someone expecting a baby, or as a unique baby-shower gift

DIFFICULTY

✂ ✂ ✂ ✂ ✂

WHAT YOU NEED

- 2.5mm hook (US C/2)
- 5.5mm (2.1in) wooden ring
- 2 plastic rattle balls
- Scissors
- Yarn needle
- Fibrefill stuffing
- 4 ply or fingering super fine cotton yarn in your chosen colours. Here we have used 1 ball each of Hobbii Rainbow Cotton in:

Colour 1: Light Grey
Colour 2: Dark Grey
Colour 3: White
Colour 4: Mint
Colour 5: Black

MEASUREMENTS

Teether: 12cm (4.7in) long; 12cm (4.7in) wide; 7cm (2.7in) deep
Rattle: 15cm (5.9in) long; 12cm (4.7in) wide; 7cm (2.7in) deep

TENSION

Is not critical for this pattern. Using 2.5mm hook with 4 ply or fingering weight yarn will create a tight stitch so that the stuffing does not show through.

PATTERN

TEETHER

HEAD

Using col 1, make a magic ring.
Rnd 1: Ch 1, work 6 dc into the ring. (6 sts)
Rnd 2: 2 dc in each st. (12 sts)
Rnd 3: (1 dc in next st, 2 dc in next st) 6 times. (18 sts)
Rnd 4: (1 dc in next 2 sts, 2 dc in next st) 6 times. (24 sts)
Rnd 5: (1 dc in next 3 sts, 2 dc in next st) 6 times. (30 sts)
Rnd 6: (1 dc in next 4 sts, 2 dc in next st) 6 times. (36 sts)
Rnd 7: (1 dc in next 5 sts, 2 dc in next st) 6 times. (42 sts)
Rnd 8: (1 dc in next 6 sts, 2 dc in next st) 6 times. (48 sts)
Rnds 9-15: 1 dc in each st. (48 sts)
Rnd 16: (1 dc in next 6 sts, dc2tog) 6 times. (42 sts)
Rnd 17: (1 dc in next 5 sts, dc2tog) 6 times. (36 sts)
Rnd 18: (1 dc in next 4 sts, dc2tog) 6 times. (30 sts)
Rnd 19: (1 dc in next 3 sts, dc2tog) 6 times. (24 sts)
Rnd 20: (1 dc in next 2 sts, dc2tog) 6 times. (18 sts)
Rnd 21: (1 dc in next st, dc2tog) 6 times. (12 sts)
Rnd 22: (Dc2tog) 6 times. (6 sts)

Fasten off and weave in ends.

NOSE

Using col 2, ch 5.
Rnd 1 (RS): 1 dc in 2nd ch from hook, 1 dc in next 2 sts, 4 dc in next st, turn and work along opposite side of the foundation chain: 1 dc in next 2 sts, 3 dc in next st. (12 sts)
Rnd 2: 2 dc in next st, 1 dc in next 3 sts, 2 dc in next st, 1 dc in next st, 2 dc in next st, 1 dc in next 3 sts, 2 dc in next st, 1 dc in next st. (16 sts)
Rnd 3: 2 dc in next st, 1 dc in next 5 sts, 2 dc in next st, 1 dc in next st, 2 dc in next st, 1 dc in next 5 sts, 2 dc in next st, 1 dc in next st. (20 sts)
Rnds 4-6: 1 dc in each st. (20 sts)

Ss in next st and fasten off, leaving a tail for sewing.

Pin and sew the nose onto the head between rnds 10 and 17.

Embroider the eyes on the head over 2 sts between rnds 10 and 11.

EARS (MAKE 2)

Using col 1, make a magic ring.
Rnd 1 (RS): Ch1, work 6 dc into the ring. (6 sts)
Rnd 2: 2 dc in each st. (12 sts)
Rnd 3: (1 dc in next st, 2 dc in next st) 6 times. (18 sts)
Rnd 4: (1 dc in next 2 sts, 2 dc in next st) 6 times. (24 sts)
Rnd 5: (1 dc in next 3 sts, 2 dc in next st) 6 times. (30 sts)

DESIGNED BY

CROCHETBYKIM

CrochetByKim is a Swedish amigurumi designer who has been making patterns since 2017. She crochets every day and sees it as a therapy for her full-time job as a 911 dispatcher.
@crochetbykim

For the teether, don't forget to place the plastic rattle ball inside the head while you crochet

Rnds 6-10: 1 dc in each st. (30 sts)
Rnd 11: (1 dc in next 3 sts, dc2tog) 6 times. (24 sts)
Rnd 12: (1 dc in next 2 sts, dc2tog) 6 times. (18 sts)

Ss in next st and fasten off, leaving a tail for sewing.

INNER EAR (MAKE 2)

Using col 3, make a magic ring.
Rnd 1 (RS): Ch 1, work 6 dc into the ring. (6 sts)
Rnd 2: 2 dc in each st. (12 sts)
Rnd 3: (1 dc in next st, 2 dc in next st) 6 times. (18 sts)

Ss in next st and fasten off, leaving a tail for sewing.

Sew the inner ears onto the ears before pinning and attaching to koala head between rnds 7 and 15.

COLLAR

Using col 4, make a magic ring.
Rnd 1 (RS): Ch 1, work 6 dc into the ring. (6 sts)
Rnd 2: 2 dc in each st. (12 sts)
Rnd 3: (1 dc in next st, 2 dc in next st) 6 times. (18 sts)
Rnd 4: (1 dc in next 2 sts, 2 dc in next st) 6 times. (24 sts)
Rnd 5: 2 dc in each st. (48 sts)
Rnd 6: (1 dc in next st, 2 dc in next st) 24 times. (72 sts)
Rnd 7: (1 dc in next st, 2 dc in next st) 36 times. (108 sts)
Rnd 8: 1 dc in each st. (108 sts)

Ss in next st and fasten off, leaving a tail for sewing.

Pin and sew rnds 3 and 4 of the collar on the underside of the koala's head.

RIBBON

Using col 1, ch 20, turn.
Row 1 (RS): 1 dc in 2nd ch from hook, 1 dc in each st to end, turn. (19 sts)
Rows 2-9: Ch 1 (does not count as a st), 1 dc in each st to end, turn. (19 sts)
Fasten off, leaving a tail for sewing.

Sew the ribbon around the wooden ring, and turn the seam to the inside of the ring. Sew the head onto the ribbon.

RATTLE
HEAD/HANDLE

Using col 1, make a magic ring and work as given for teether Head up to the end of row 20. (18 sts)
Rnd 21: In front loops only, 1 dc in each st. (18 sts)

Stuff the head and put bell inside. Continue stuffing as you go along.

Rnds 22-34: 1 dc in each st. (18 sts)
Rnd 35: (1 dc in next 2 sts, 2 dc in next st) 6 times. (24 sts)
Rnd 36: (1 dc in next 3 sts, 2 dc in next st) 6 times. (30 sts)
Rnds 37-41: 1 dc in each st. (30 sts)
Rnd 42: (1 dc in next 3 sts, dc2tog) 6 times. (24 sts)
Rnd 43: (1 dc in next 2 sts, dc2tog) 6 times. (18 sts)
Rnd 44: (1 dc in next st, dc2tog) 6 times. (12 sts)
Rnd 45: (Dc2tog) 6 times. (6 sts)

Fasten off, leaving a tail for sewing.

NOSE

Using col 2, work as given for teether nose.

Pin and sew the nose onto the head between rnds 10 and 17.

Embroider the eyes on the head over 2 sts between rnds 10 and 11.

EARS (MAKE 2)

Using col 1, work as given for teether ears.

INNER EAR (MAKE 2)

Using col 3, work as given for teether inner ears.

Sew inner ears to ears before pinning and attaching to rattle between rnds 7 and 15.

PATCH

Using col 3, ch 7.
Rnd 1 (RS): 1 dc in 2nd ch from hook, 1 dc in next 4 sts, 4 dc in next st. Turn and work along opposite side of the foundation chain: 1 dc in next 4 sts, 3 dc in next st. (16 sts)
Rnd 2: 2 dc in next st, 1 dc in next 5 sts, 2 dc in next st, 1 dc in next st, 2 dc in next st, 1 dc in next 5 sts, 2 dc in next st, 1 dc in next st. (20 sts)

Ss in next st and fasten off, leaving a tail for sewing.

Pin and sew patch to rattles between rnds 22 and 31 on handle.

PATTERN NOTES

- Work in the round without turning or joining. Using a stitch marker to mark the beginning of each round will make it easier to keep track of which round you're working on.

Hot air balloon mobile

This adorable hot air balloon mobile would make a charming addition to any nursery

DIFFICULTY

✂ ✂ ✂ ✂ ✂

WHAT YOU NEED

- 4mm hook (US G/6)
- Yarn needle
- Scissors
- Stitch marker
- Fibrefill stuffing
- Mobile frame
- Cotton aran weight yarn in your chosen colours. Here we have used I Love This Cotton! in:

Colour 1: Curry (11g)
Colour 2: Glowing (3g)
Colour 3: Black (oddments)
Colour 4: Strawberry Violet (14g)
Colour 5: Mango (14g)
Colour 6: Deep Teal (14g)
Colour 7: Apple Green (14g)
Colour 8: Brown (12.5g)
Colour 9: Mulberry (oddments)
Colour 10: Coral (oddments)
Colour 11: Bright Green (oddments)
Colour 12: Aqua (oddments)

MEASUREMENTS

Sun: 11.5cm (4.5in) tall
Hot air balloon: 10cm (4in) tall

TENSION

9 sts and 10 rounds to measure 5x5cm (2x2in) over double crochet, using 4mm hook and aran weight yarn

SPECIAL STITCHES:

Double crochet back loop only (dcblo): rather than inserting your hook through both loops of the top of the stitch as normal, insert your hook into the back loop only and complete your dc.

PATTERN

SMILEY SUN

Using col 1, make a magic ring.
Rnd 1 (RS): Work 6 dc into magic ring. (6 sts)
Rnd 2: 2 dc in each st. (12 sts)
Rnd 3: (2 dc in next st, 1 dc in next st) 6 times. (18 sts)
Rnd 4: (2 dc in next st, 1 dc in next 2 sts) 6 times. (24 sts)
Rnd 5: (2 dc in next st, 1 dc in next 3 sts) 6 times. (30 sts)
Rnd 6: 1 dc in each st. (30 sts)
Rnd 7: (2 dc in next st, 1 dc in next 4 sts) 6 times. (36 sts)
Rnds 8-9: 1 dc in each st. (36 sts)
Rnd 10: 1 dc in the back loop of each st. (36 sts)
Rnd 11: 1 dc in each st. (36 sts)
Rnd 12: (Dc2tog, 1 dc in next 4 sts) 6 times. (30 sts)
Rnd 13: 1 dc in each st. (30 sts)

Place a stitch marker in the loop on your hook to hold your place and remove from your hook.

Using col 2: Ray Rnd 1: Make a standing dc in 1st remaining front loop leftover from rnd 10, (1 dc in next front loop) 33 times, dc2tog across the last 2 front loops, ss in first dc to join. (35 sts)
Ray Rnd 2: (Ch 5, ss in 2nd ch from hook, 1 dc in next ch, 1 htr in next ch, 1 tr in last ch, sk next 2 sts of Ray Rnd 1 and ss in the 3rd st to join, ch 6, ss in 2nd ch from hook, 1 dc in next ch, 1 htr in next ch, 1 tr in next ch, 1 dtr in the last ch, sk next 3 sts of Ray Rnd 2 and ss in the 4th st to join) 5 times, ss in base of beginning ch 5 to join.
Fasten off.

Using the yarn needle and Yarn 3, stitch French knots for the eyes between rnds 3 and 4, then stitch a smiling mouth between rnds 5 and 6.

Begin stuffing and continue to stuff as you go.

Place col 1 back onto your hook and remove the stitch marker.
Rnd 14: (Dc2tog, 1 dc in next 3 sts) 6 times. (24 sts)

DESIGNED BY

ERIN SHARP

Erin is an avid crocheter and crafter who runs the blog The Cookie Snob. Her biggest crochet inspirations are her three children and their growing imaginations.
www.cookiesnobcrochet.com
www.facebook.com/CookieSnobCrochet

You will end up with 4 'ropes' tethering your balloon to your basket

Rnd 15: (Dc2tog, 1 dc in next 2 sts) 6 times. (18 sts)
Rnd 16: (Dc2tog, 1 dc in next st) 6 times. (12 sts)
Rnd 17: (Dc2tog) 6 times. (6 sts)

Finish stuffing. Fasten off, leaving a yarn tail. Using a yarn needle, weave the yarn tail through the front loop of the remaining sts and pull to close. Weave in ends.

BALLOON

Using col 4, make a magic ring.
Rnd 1 (RS): Ch 1, work 6 dc into magic ring, ss in beginning ch 1 to join. (6 sts)
Rnd 2: Ch 1, 2 dc in each st, ss in ch 1 to join. (12 sts)
Rnd 3: Ch 1, (2 dc in next st, 1 dc in next st) 6 times, ss in ch 1 to join. (18 sts)
Rnd 4: Ch 1, (2 dc in next st, 1 dc in next 2 sts) 6 times, ss in ch 1 to join. (24 sts)
Rnd 5: Ch 1, (2 dc in next st, 1 dc in next 3 sts) 6 times, ss in ch 1 to join. (30 sts)
Rnd 6: Ch 1, 1 dc in each st, ss in ch 1 to join. (30 sts)
Rnd 7: Ch 1, (2 dc in next st, 1 dc in next 4 sts) 6 times, ss in ch 1 to join. (36 sts)
Rnds 8-11: Ch 1, 1 dc in each st, ss in ch 1 to join. (36 sts)
Rnd 12: Ch 1, (dc2tog, 1 dc in next 4 sts) 6 times, ss in ch 1 to join. (30 sts)
Rnd 13: Ch 1, 1 dc in each st, ss in ch 1 to join. (30 sts)
Rnd 14: Ch 1, (dc2tog, 1 dc in next 3 sts) 6 times, ss in ch 1 to join. (24 sts)
Rnd 15: Ch 1, 1 dc in each st, ss in ch 1 to join. (24 sts)
Rnd 16: Ch 1, (dc2tog, 1 dc in next 2 sts) 6 times, ss in ch 1 to join. (18 sts)
Rnd 17: Ch 1, 1 dc in each st, ss in ch 1 to join. (18 sts)
Begin stuffing with the toy filing. Continue to stuff as you go.
Rnd 18: Ch 1, (dc2tog, 1 dc in next st) 6 times, ss in ch 1 to join. (12 sts)
Rnd 19: Ch 1, 1 dc in each st, ss in ch 1 to join. (12 sts)
Rnd 20: Ch 1, (dc2togblo) 6 times, ss to ch 1 to join. (6 sts)

Finish stuffing. Fasten off, leaving a yarn tail. Using a yarn needle, weave the yarn tail through the front loop of the remaining sts and pull to close. Weave in ends.

Rep with cols 5, 6 and 7. You should now have 4 different coloured balloons.

BASKET (MAKE 4)

Using col 8, make a magic ring.
Rnd 1 (RS): Ch 1, work 6 dc into magic ring, ss in beginning ch 1 to join. (6 sts)
Rnd 2: Ch 1, 2 dc in each st, ss in ch 1 to join. (12 sts)
Rnds 3-5: Ch 1, 1 dc blo in each st, ss in ch 1 to join. (12 sts)
Fasten off, leaving an extra-long tail.

The balloons can be made in any colour combinations you prefer and will still look great. If you prefer a more uniform look, you can even make them all the same colour

DECORATION AND ASSEMBLY

Using the yarn needle and col 9, stitch the balloon panel design onto the balloon made with col 4. Start by stitching 6 small sections (3 sts long each) between rnds 3 and 4 (at the top), to form a circle. Then stitch the long vertical lines from the circle you just made all the way down to the bottom of the balloon. There should be 6 vertical lines, spaced evenly (about 3 sts apart from each other at the top and about 2 sts apart from each other at the bottom). For extra definition, stitch 6 small sections (2 sts long each) at the very bottom of the balloon between rnds 19 and 20, to form another small circle. Weave in ends.

Repeat this process to decorate the balloon made with col 5 using col 10. Then decorate the balloon made with col 6 using col 11 and the balloon made with col 7 using col 12 in the same manner.

To attach the basket, use the yarn needle and the long yarn tail left over from making the basket. Thread the tail through the base of the balloon, leaving a 2.5cm (1in) gap between the basket and the balloon. Make a small knot to keep everything in place. Then weave the yarn tail through the balloon base for a few stitches and then thread the tail back into the basket, a few stitches apart from where you started, leaving another 2.5cm (1in) gap. Knot to secure and weave the yarn tail through the top of the basket for a few stitches. Repeat this process until you have 4 'ropes' tethering your balloon to your basket. Fasten off and weave in any remaining ends. Repeat this process until each balloon has a basket attached to it.

Repeat the decoration and assembly process for each balloon. Once all your mobile pieces are ready, thread a bit of matching yarn through the top of each piece and use it to attach each piece to your frame with the sun in the middle and one hot air balloon on each arm.

PATTERN NOTES

- The sun is worked in the round without turning or joining. Using a stitch marker to mark the beginning of each round will make it easier to keep track of which round you're working on.

Sherbet stripes blanket

Candy-coloured rainbows and lots of cosy texture, this baby blanket has it all!

DIFFICULTY

✂ ✂ ✂ ✂ ✂

WHAT YOU NEED

- 4.5mm hook (US 7)
- Yarn needle
- Scissors
- Piece of thick card 16cm (6¼in) wide, to make tassels
- Aran yarn in your chosen colours. Here we have used 1 ball each of Paintbox Simply Aran in:

Colour 1: Tea Rose
Colour 2: Bubblegum
Colour 3: Peach Orange
Colour 4: Daffodil Yellow
Colour 5: Pistachio Green
Colour 6: Spearmint Green
Colour 7: Seafoam Blue
Colour 8: Washed Teal
Colour 9: Dolphin Blue (Border Colour)

MEASUREMENTS

The finished blanket measures approximately 80 x 90cm (31½ x 35½in) including border

TENSION

15.5 sts and 13 rows to measure 10 x 10cm (4 x 4in) over pattern, using 4.5mm hook

SPECIAL STITCHES:

Cluster – In this pattern the cluster stitches are made by joining 4 treble stitches together as follows: yarn over and work the first treble stitch but stop when you have two loops left on your hook. Leave these last two loops on your hook and then repeat this process again, working a treble into the next stitch but leaving the last two loops on your hook (you now have 3 loops on your hook). Repeat over the next two stitches until you have 5 loops on your hook, yarn over and pull through all 5 loops. To work a cluster in the ch3 sp, you work all 4 stitches into the ch3 sp.

PATTERN

Using col 1, ch 117.

Row 1 (RS): 1 dc in 2nd ch from hook, *3 ch, cl over next 4 ch, 1 ch, 1 dc in next ch; rep from * to end, change to colour 2, turn.

Row 2: Ch 3, *1 dc in top of cl, 3 ch, cl in 3ch-sp, 1 ch; rep from * to last st, 1 dc in last st, change to colour 3, turn.

Row 3: Ch 3, *1 dc in top of cl, 3 ch, cl in 3ch-sp, 1 ch; rep from * to 3ch-sp at end, 1 dc in 3ch-sp, change to colour 4, turn.

Row 3 forms the pattern.

Rep row 3, changing colour at the end of each row until you have finished the colour repeat (cols 1-8). There are 8 repeats of this stripe sequence in the blanket pictured; if you are making a bigger blanket you will need to continue until you get to your desired size. Fasten off on the last row and weave in all ends before beginning the border.

BORDER

Rnd 1 (RS): Using col 8, with RS facing, join yarn in any stitch with a ss, ch2 (counts as a st), htr around the blanket edge, working (2 htr, 2 ch, 2 htr) in each corner, ss in the top of the beginning ch2.

TIP: evenly space your htr stitches in Rnd 1 to prevent the blanket from warping.

Rnd 2: 1 ch, 1 dcblo in each st around the blanket edge and (2 dc, 2 ch, 2 dc) in each corner, ss in beginning ch and fasten off.

Rnds 3-7: Use colours in the following order: 5, 4, 3, 2 & 1. Attach yarn to any corner ch2-sp using a ss, 1 ch (does not count as a st), 1 dc in each st, all around blanket edge and (1 dc, 2 ch, 1 dc) in corner spaces, ss in beginning ch, fasten off.

TIP: When working rnds 3 to 7, fasten off at the end of each rnd then start the next colour in a different corner. This gives a neater finish.

Rnd 8: Using col 8, join yarn in any corner ch2-sp, ch2, 1 htr in each st around blanket edge (2htr, ch2, 2htr) in each corner, ss in top of beginning 2 ch, fasten off and sew in ends.

DESIGNED BY

KATE ROWELL

Kate is a crochet designer based in Cambridgeshire, UK. She enjoys working with simple stitches, texture and lots of bright colours.
@jellybean_junction
blog.jellybeanjunction.co.uk

TIP: Because you have worked several rounds of double crochets, the blanket may not sit completely flat. This can be rectified by gently pulling it flat and then blocking with water.

TASSELS

Using all colours held together and a piece of thick card, make 4 tassels and attach one to each corner.

PATTERN NOTES

- To make a bigger blanket, you can adjust the starting chain – just ensure that the chain is always a multiple of 5+2.

Playroom

50
Fox puppet

54
Amigurumi food

60
Sleepy sheep

62
Little dress-up doll

66
Octopus hand puppet

70
Giant mouse

74
Football captain

78
Horace the monster

82
Little bunny

84
Trio of dinosaurs

94
Gelato rainbow basket

98
Ripples wall hanging

Fox puppet

This playful and cute crochet puppet will melt any little one's heart

DIFFICULTY

✂ ✂ ✂ ✂ ✂

WHAT YOU NEED

- 5mm hook (US H/8)
- Yarn needle
- Fibrefill stuffing
- 15mm gold and black safety eyes
- Chunky yarn in any colours. Here we have used Durable Cosy in:

Colour 1: Black (1 ball)
Colour 2: Orange (2 balls)
Colour3: White (1 ball)

MEASUREMENTS

24cm (9in) long (excluding tail), 12cm (5in) wide

TENSION

Is not critical

PATTERN

PUPPET BASE:

With col 1, start with a magic ring.

Rnd 1 (RS): Ch 1, work 6 dc into the ring. (6 sts)

Rnd 2: 2 dc in each st. (12 sts)

Rnd 3: (1 dc in next st, 2 dc in next) 3 times, 1 dc in next st, change to col 2, 2 dc in next st, change to col 3, (1 dc in next st, 2 dc in next st) twice. (18 sts)

Fasten off col 1.

Rnd 4: (1 dc in next 2 sts, 2 dc in next st) 3 times, 1 dc in next st, change to col 2, 1 dc in next st, 2 dc in next, 1 dc in next st, change to col 3, 1 dc in next st, 2 dc in next, 1 dc in next 2 sts, 2 dc in next st. (24 sts)

Rnd 5: (1 dc in next 3 sts, 2 dc in next st) 3 times, 1 dc in next st, change to col 2, 1 dc in next 2 sts, 2 dc in next, 1 dc in next 2 sts, change to col 3, 1 dc in next st, 2 dc in next, 1 dc in next 3 sts, 2 dc in next st. (30 sts)

DESIGNED BY

SASCHA BLASE-VAN WAGTEN-DONK

Sascha Blase is a Dutch pattern designer known as 'A la Sascha'. She has written ten Dutch crochet books and is currently working on her eleventh. Her bestseller, *Crochet Ragdolls*, is now available in English. **@alasascha**

Rnd 6: (1 dc in next 4 sts, 2 dc in next st) 3 times, 1 dc in next st, change to col 2, 1 dc in next 3 sts, 2 dc in next st, 1 dc in next 3 sts, change to col 3, 1 dc in next st, 2 dc in next st, 1 dc in next 4 sts, 2 dc in next st. (36 sts)
Rnd 7: 1 dc in next 19 sts, change to col 2, 1 dc in next 9 sts, change to col 3, 1 dc in next 8 sts. (36 sts)
Rnd 8: 1 dc in next 19 sts, change to col 2, 1 dc in next 10 sts, change to col 3, 1 dc in next 7 sts. (36 sts)
Rnd 9: 1 dc in next 19 sts, change to col 2, 1 dc in next 11 sts, change to col 3, 1 dc in next 6 sts. (36 sts)
Rnd 10: 1 dc in next 19 sts, change to col 2, 1 dc in next 12 sts, change to col 3, 1 dc in next 5 sts. (36 sts)
Rnd 11: 1 dc in next 19 sts, change to col 2, 1 dc in next 17 sts. (36 sts)
Fasten off col 3.
Rnds 12-19: 1 dc in each st. (36 sts)
Rnd 20: 1 dc in next 2 sts, ch 12, sk next 12 sts (for mouth), 1 dc in next 22 sts. (36 sts)
Rnd 21: 1 dc in each st and ch. (36 sts)
Rnds 22-40: 1 dc in each st. (36 sts)
Fasten off and weave in ends.

MOUTH

Rnd 1: With col 2, starting at first skipped stitch of rnd 20, 1 dc in each skipped st and in each ch of rnd 20. (24 sts)
Rnds 2-9: 1 dc in each st. (24 sts)
Rnd 10: Change to col 3, 1 dc in each st. (24 sts)
Fasten off col 2.
Rnd 11: (1 dc in next 4 sts, dc2tog) to end. (20 sts)
Rnd 12: (1 dc in next 3 sts, dc2tog) to end. (16 sts)
Rnd 13: (1 dc in next 2 sts, dc2tog) to end. (12 sts)
Rnd 14: (1 dc in next st, dc2tog) to end. (8 sts)

Cut yarn and fasten off. Weave through 8 remaining stitches and pull tight to close the gap; weave in ends.

EARS (MAKE 2)

With col 1, start with a magic ring.
Rnd 1 (RS): Ch 1, work 6dc in the ring. (6 sts)
Rnd 2: (1 dc in next st, 2 dc in next st) to end. (9 sts)
Rnd 3: Change to col 2, 1 dc in each st. (9 sts)
Fasten off col 1.
Rnd 4: (1 dc in next 2 sts, 2 dc in next st) to end. (12 sts)
Rnd 5: 1 dc in each st. (12 sts)
Rnd 6: (1 dc in next 3 sts, 2 dc in next st) to end. (15 sts)
Rnd 7: 1 dc in each st. (15)
Rnd 8: (1 dc in next 4 sts, 2 dc in next st) to end. (18 sts)
Rnd 9: 1 dc in each st. (18 sts)
Fasten off, leaving a long tail to attach ears on each side of the head between rnds 17-18, 4 stitches apart. It's easiest to determine exact placement when folded flat and placed on a surface. Take the safety eyes and insert them between rnds 12-13 on each side of the head, 7 stitches apart.

TAIL

With col 3, start with a magic ring.
Rnd 1 (RS): Ch 1, work 6dc into the ring. (6 sts)
Rnd 2: (1 dc in next st, 2 dc in next st) to end. (9 sts)
Rnd 3: 1 dc in each st. (9 sts)
Rnd 4: (1 dc in next 2 sts, 2 dc in next st) to end. (12 sts)
Rnd 5: 1 dc in each st. (12 sts)
Rnd 6: (1 dc in next 3 sts, 2 dc in next st) to end. (15 sts)
Rnd 7: Change to col 2, 1 dc in each st. (15 sts)
Fasten off col 3.
Rnd 8: (1 dc in next 4 sts, 2 dc in next st) to end. (18 sts)
Rnd 9: (1 dc in next 5 sts, 2 dc in next st) to end. (21 sts)
Rnds 10-12: 1 dc in each st. (21 sts)
Rnd 13: (1 dc in next 5 sts, dc2tog) to end. (18 sts)
Rnd 14: 1 dc in each st. (18 sts)
Rnd 15: (1 dc in next 4 sts, dc2tog) to end. (15 sts)
Rnd 16: 1 dc in each st. (15 sts)
Rnd 17: (1 dc in next 3 sts, dc2tog) to end. (12 sts)
Rnd 18: 1 dc in each st. (12 sts)
Stuff the tail lightly with fibrefill.
Rnd 19: (Dc2tog) to end. (6 sts)
Fasten off and weave yarn through 6 remaining stitches and pull tight to close the gap but leave a long yarn tail, to attach tail in the center of the base between rnds 36-38.

"There is something rather charming about this little woodland creature"

PATTERN NOTES

- Most pieces are worked in a spiral, in continuous rounds. Using a stitch marker in the first stitch of each round is the easiest way to keep track of the start of each round.
- The neatest way to change colour is to complete the last step of previous stitch with the new colour, for example: if the last stitch before the change is a dc, the last yarn over hook and pull through 2 loops will be with the new colour.

Amigurumi food

This set is the perfect treat for any child – and the pieces work up quickly, too

DIFFICULTY

✂ ✂ ✂ ✂ ✂

WHAT YOU NEED

- 2.75mm or 3mm hook (US C/2)
- Embroidery needle
- Embroidery thread in pink, black, green and white
- Fibrefill stuffing
- Stitch marker
- Yarn needle
- Two 6mm black toy safety eyes for each item
- You will need to use aran weight yarn in your chosen colours. We have used Lion Brand Vanna's Choice in:

Colour 1: Red
Colour 2: White
Colour 3: Brown
Colour 4: Light yellow
Colour 5: Green
Colour 6: Soft white
Colour 7: Cornmeal yellow
Colour 8: Rust
Colour 9: Beige
Colour 10: Light brown
Colour 11: Golden
Colour 12: Lime
Colour 13: Purple
Colour 14: Honey

MEASUREMENTS

Mini soda fresh cola: 15cm (6in)
Ketchup: 12cm (4¾in)
Mini hot dog: 10cm (4in)
Mini burger: 9cm (3½in)
Mini toast: 8cm (3in)

SPECIAL STITCHES

Crab stitch: worked as a regular dc stitch, but working into the stitch to the right of your hook, rather than the left.

Chain stitch (embroidery): Insert the embroidery needle from the back and pull thread through. * Re-insert the needle through the fabric as if to make one small running stitch (and bringing the needle out just a short distance along), then place the thread behind the needle. Pull the needle through to create a chain stitch (do not pull too tightly – leave the thread loose). To continue the chain, rep from *, each time inserting the needle back into same place and out again a little further along. Keep going as needed.

PATTERN

MINI SODA FRESH COLA BOTTLE

Using col 3, make a magic ring.
Rnd 1 (RS): 6 dc in magic ring and pull ring tight to close. (6 sts)
Rnd 2: 2 dc in each st. (12 sts)
Rnd 3: (1 dc in next st, 2 dc in next st) 6 times. (18 sts)
Rnd 4: (1 dc in next 2 sts, 2 dc in next st) 6 times. (24 sts)
Rnd 5: (1 dc in next 3 sts, 2 dc in next st) 6 times. (30 sts)
Rnd 6: 1 dc in back loop of each st. (30 sts)
Rnd 7: 1 dc in each st. (30 sts)
Rnd 8: (1 dc in next 3 sts, dc2tog) 6 times. (24 sts)
Rnd 9: 1 dc in each st. (24 sts)
Rnd 10: (1 dc in next 2 sts, dc2tog) 6 times. (18 sts)
Rnd 11: (1 dc in next 2 sts, 2 dc in next st) 6 times. (24 sts)
Rnd 12: (1 dc in next 3 sts, 2 dc in next st) 6 times. (30 sts)
In last st of last rnd, change to col 1.
Rnd 13: 1 dc in each st. (30 sts)
In last st of last rnd, change to col 2.
Rnd 14: 1 dc in each st. (30 sts)
In last st of last rnd, change to col 1.
Rnds 15-18: 1 dc in each st. (30 sts)
Place safety eyes between rnds 16-17.
Embroider cheeks on each side of eyes, by making three horizontal

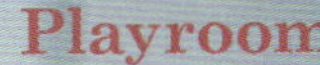

DESIGNED BY

ANNERIS KONDRATAS

Anneris is an illustrator and a crochet designer who lives in Virginia with her husband and two sons. Everything started as a hobby, writing a blog about food characters that she called Amigurumi Food. Since 2015 she has been selling her creations and patterns on Etsy.
@amigurumifood
www.etsy.com/shop/Amigurumifood

PATTERN NOTES

- Most pieces are worked in a spiral, without joining each round. It may help to use a stitch marker to mark the first stitch of the round, and move it up as you work each round.

- To change colour in last st of rnd, work your stitch until there are two loops left on hook, drop yarn and work the last yoh in new colour and pull a loop through. New colour is on hook, ready to start next rnd in that colour.

backstitches with pink thread.
Embroider mouth beneath the eyes, by making two diagonal backstitches with black thread.
Change to col 2.
Rnd 19: 1 dc in each st. (30 sts)
In last st of last rnd, change to col 1.
Rnd 20: 1 dc in each st. (30 sts)
In last st of last rnd, change to col 3.
Rnd 21: (1 dc in next 3 sts, dc2tog) 6 times. (24 sts)
Rnd 22: 1 dc in each st. (24 sts)
Rnd 23: (1 dc in next 2 sts, dc2tog) 6 times. (18 sts)
Fill the bottle with fibrefill stuffing.
Rnd 24: (1 dc in next st, dc2tog) 6 times. (12 sts)
Rnd 25: 1 dc in each st. (12 sts)
In last st of last rnd, change to col 2.
Rnd 26: 1 dc in each st. (12 sts)
Rnd 27: 1 crab stitch in each st. (12 sts)
Sl st in first st and fasten off.

STRAW

Using col 2, make a magic ring.
Rnd 1 (RS): 6 dc in magic ring and pull tight to close. (6 sts)
Rnds 2-5: 1 dc in each st. (6 sts)
In last st of last rnd, change to col 4.
Rnds 6-9: 1 dc in each st. (6 sts)
In last st of last rnd, change to col 2.
Rnd 10: 1 dc in each st. (6 sts)
Sl st in next st and fasten off, leaving a long tail for sewing. No stuffing is needed.

ASSEMBLY

Place the straw inside the bottle, following the position with the photo tutorial. Sew rnd 10 of the straw to rnd 26 of the bottle.

KETCHUP LABEL

Using col 2, ch 4.
Rnd 1: 2 dc in 2nd chain from hook, 1 dc in next ch, 4 dc in last ch, rotate and work along the opposite side of the chains, 1 dc in next ch, 2 dc in last ch. (10 sts)
Continue to work in a spiral.
Rnd 2: 2 dc in first st, 2 dc in next st, 1 dc in next st, 2 dc in next 4 sts, 1 dc in next st, 2 dc in next 2 sts. (18 sts)
Sl st in next st and fasten off, leaving a long tail for sewing.
Embroider a chain stitch around the edge of the label with green thread.
Place the safety eyes in the centre and embroider the mouth with black thread.

BOTTLE

Using col 1, make a magic ring.
Rnd 1 (RS): 6 dc in magic ring and pull tight to close. (6 sts)
Rnd 2: 2 dc in each st. (12 sts)
Rnd 3: (1 dc in next st, 2 dc in next st) 6 times. (18 sts)
Rnd 4: (1 dc in next 2 sts, 2 dc in next st) 6 times. (24 sts)
Rnd 5: (1 dc in next 3 sts, 2 dc in next st) 6 times. (30 sts)
Rnd 6: 1 dc in back loop of each st. (30 sts)
Rnd 7-16: 1 dc in each st. (30 sts)
Rnd 17: (1 dc in next 3 sts, dc2tog) 6 times. (24 sts)
Rnd 18: 1 dc in each st. (24 sts)

Rnd 19: (1 dc in next 2 sts, dc2tog) 6 times. (18 sts)
Sew the label between rnds 14 and 18.
Rnds 20-21: 1 dc in each st. (18 sts)
Rnd 22: (1 dc in next st, dc2tog) 6 times. (12 sts)
Place the fibrefill stuffing inside the piece.
Rnd 23: 1 dc in each st. (12 sts)
In last st of last rnd, change to col 2.
Rnd 24: 1 dc in each st. (12 sts)
In last st of last rnd, change to col 5.
Rnd 25: 1 dc in each st. (12 sts)
In last st of last rnd, change to col 1.
Rnds 26-27: 1 dc in each st. (12 sts)
Rnd 28: 1 dc in back loop of each st. (12 sts)
Rnd 29: (dc2tog) 6 times. (6 sts)
Sl st in next st and fasten off.

TOP

Using col 2, make a magic ring.
Rnd 1 (RS): 6 dc in magic ring and pull tight to close. (6 sts)
Rnd 2: 2 dc in each st. (12 sts)
Rnd 3: 1 dc in back loop of each st. (12 sts)
Rnd 4: Sl st in each st. (12 sts)
Fasten off.

ASSEMBLY

Sew the top to the bottle.

MINI HOT DOG: OUTSIDE BUN (MAKE 2)

Using col 7, ch 15.
Rnd 1 (RS): 2 dc in 2nd chain from hook, 1 dc in next 12 sts, 3 dc in last st, rotate and work along opposite side of chains, 1 dc in next 12 ch, 1 dc in last ch. (30 sts)

Continue to work in a spiral.
Rnd 2: 2 dc in first st, 2 dc in next st, 1 dc in next 12 sts, 2 dc in next 3 sts, 1 dc in next 12 sts, 2 dc in last st. (36 sts)
Rnds 3-4: 1 dc in each st. (36 sts)
Sl st in next st, fasten off and leave a long tail for sewing.

INSIDE BUN (MAKE 2)

Using col 6, ch 15.
Rnd 1 (RS): 2 dc in 2nd chain from hook, 1 dc in next 12 ch, 3 dc in last ch, rotate and work along opposite side of chains, 1 dc in next 12 ch, 1 dc in last ch. (30 sts)
Continue to work in a spiral.
Rnd 2: 2 dc in first st, 2 dc in next st, 1 dc in next 12 sts, 2 dc in next 3 sts, 1 dc in next 12 sts, 2 dc in last st. (36 sts)
Sl st in next st and fasten off.

HOT DOG

Using col 8, make a magic ring.
Rnd 1 (RS): 6 dc in magic ring and pull tight to close. (6 sts)
Rnd 2: 2 dc in each st. (12 sts)
Rnds 3-7: 1 dc in each st. (12 sts)
Place safety eyes in rnd 6. Embroider mouth and cheeks with black and pink thread.

Rnds 8-19: 1 dc in each st. (12 sts)
Stuff with fibrefill stuffing.
Rnd 20: (dc2tog) 6 times. (6 sts)
Sl st in next st and fasten off.

ASSEMBLY

Sew the two buns together, right sides facing out. For the ketchup swirl, ch 20 in col 1, leaving a long tail. Sew the strip of ketchup to the hot dog in a zigzag pattern. Using col 7, secure the hot dog between the buns.

MINI BURGER: OUTSIDE BUN (MAKE 2)

Using col 9, make a magic ring.
Rnd 1 (RS): 6 dc in magic ring and pull tight to close. (6 sts)
Rnd 2: 2 dc in each st. (12 sts)
Rnd 3: (1 dc in next st, 2 dc in next st) 6 times. (18 sts)
Rnd 4: (1 dc in next st, 2 dc in next st) 6 times. (24 sts)
Rnd 5: (1 dc in next 3 sts, 2 dc in next st) 6 times. (30 sts)
Rnd 6: (1 dc in next 4 sts, 2 dc in next st) 6 times. (36 sts)
Rnds 7-8: 1 dc in each st. (36 sts)
Sl st in next st and fasten off, leaving a long tail for sewing.
Place safety eyes in rnd 6, leaving a small gap in between them. Embroider mouth with black thread making two diagonal backstitches. Embroider cheeks with pink thread by making 3 horizontal backstitches. Embroider sesame seeds on top of the bun by making one backstitch with double thread in warm yellow.

INSIDE BUN (MAKE 2)

Using col 6, make a magic ring.
Rnd 1 (RS): 6 dc in magic ring and pull tight to close. (6 sts)
Rnd 2: 2 dc in each st. (12 sts)
Rnd 3: (1 dc in next st, 2 dc in next st) 6 times. (18 sts)
Rnd 4: (1 dc in next st, 2 dc in next st) 6 times. (24 sts)
Rnd 5: (1 dc in next 3 sts, 2 dc in next st) 6 times. (30 sts)
Rnd 6: (1 dc in next 4 sts, 2 dc in next st) 6 times. (36 sts)
Sl st in next st and fasten off.

BURGER PATTY

Using col 10, make magic ring.
Rnd 1 (RS): 6 dc in magic ring and pull tight to close. (6 sts)
Rnd 2: 2 dc in each st. (12 sts)
Rnd 3: (1 dc in next st, 2 dc in next st) 6 times. (18 sts)
Rnd 4: (1 dc in next st, 2 dc in next st) 6 times. (24 sts)
Rnd 5: (1 dc in next 3 sts, 2 dc in next st) 6 times. (30 sts)
Rnd 6: (1 dc in next 4 sts, 2 dc in next st) 6 times. (36 sts)
Rnd 7: 1 dc in each st. (36 sts)
Rnd 8: (1 dc in next 4 sts, dc2tog) 6 times. (30 sts)
Rnd 9: (1 dc in next 3 sts, dc2tog) 6 times. (24 sts)
Rnd 10: (1 dc in next 2 sts, dc2tog) 6 times. (18 sts)
Rnd 11: (1 dc in next st, dc2tog) 6 times. (12 sts)
Rnd 12: (dc2tog) 6 times. (6 sts)
Sl st in next st and fasten off. No stuffing is needed.

LETTUCE

Using col 12, make a magic ring.
Rnd 1 (RS): 6 dc in magic ring and pull tight to close. (6 sts)
Rnd 2: 2 dc in each st. (12 sts)
Rnd 3: (1 dc in next st, 2 dc in next st) 6 times. (18 sts)
Rnd 4: (1 dc in next 2 sts, 2 dc in next st) 6 times. (24 sts)
Rnd 5: (1 dc in next 3 sts, 2 dc in next st) 6 times. (30 sts)
Rnd 6: (1 dc in next 4 sts, 2 dc in next st) 6 times. (36 sts)
Rnd 7: *(1 tr and 1 dtr) in next st, (1 dtr and 1 tr) in next st, sl st in next st; rep from * 11 times more. (60 sts)
Fasten off and weave in ends.

CHEESE

Using col 11, ch 12.
Row 1: 1 dc in 2nd chain from hook, 1 dc in each of next 10 ch, turn. (11 sts).
Rows 2-8: Ch 1 (does not count as a st), 1 dc in each st to end, turn. (11 sts).
Do not fasten off, continue to work a border around the cheese, by working 1 dc in same st (to make a corner), work 1 dc in each st or row-end and 2 dc in each corner, then when you reach the end, sl st in first dc and fasten off.

TOMATO SLICE

Using col 1, make a magic ring.
Rnd 1 (RS): 6 dc in magic ring and pull tight to close. (6 sts)

Rnd 2: 2 dc in each st. (12 sts)
Rnd 3: (1 dc in next st, 2 dc in next st) 6 times. (18 sts)
Rnd 4: (1 dc in next 2 sts, 2 dc in next st) 6 times. (24 sts)
Rnd 5: (1 dc in next 3 sts, 2 dc in next st) 6 times. (30 sts)
Rnd 6: Sl st in first st, ch 3 (counts as first tr), 1 tr in next 3 sts, ch 2, skip 1 st, (1 tr in next 4 sts, ch 2, skip 1 st) 5 times. Sl st to top of beginning ch 3 and fasten off. (30 tr and 6 ch2-sps)

ASSEMBLY

Sew the two buns together, with right sides facing out. Stuff with fibrefill before closing. Sew all of the pieces together using col 9, through the middle of each one in the following order: bottom bun, lettuce, tomato, burger, cheese, top bun. Secure all parts to the top bun.

TOAST (MAKE 2)

Using col 9, ch 13.
Row 1 (RS): 1 dc in 2nd chain from hook, 1 dc in next 11 ch, turn. (12 sts)
Rows 2-10: Ch 1 (does not count as a st throughout), 1 dc in each st to end, turn. (12 sts)
Row 11: Ch 1, 2 dc in first st, 1 dc in each st to last st, 2 dc in last st, turn. (14 sts)
Row 12: As Row 11. (16 sts)
Row 13: As Row 11 but do not turn at end. (18 sts)
Fasten off.
With RS facing, join col 14 with a sl st to last st, and ch 1.
Edging rnd: 2 dc in same st, then work dc around the edge of the toast, by working 1 dc in each st or row-end and 2 dc in each corner. Sl st in first dc and fasten off, leaving a long tail for sewing.

JELLY/PEANUT BUTTER

Using col 13 (for jelly) or col 11 (for peanut butter), make a magic ring.
Rnd 1 (RS): 6 dc in magic ring and pull tight to close. (6 sts)
Rnd 2: 2 dc in each st. (12 sts)
Rnd 3: (2 tr in next 4 sts, sl st in same st as last 2 tr) twice, 2 htr in next 4 sts, sl st in same st as last 2 htr, sl st in top of first tr. Fasten off, leaving a long tail for sewing.

ASSEMBLY

Place safety eyes between rnds 1 and 2 of the jelly/peanut butter part. Embroider cheeks with pink and mouth with white thread. Sew the jelly and peanut butter to one slice of toast. Place and sew the slices of toast together working with col 10 and 14 through the edge.

DESIGNED BY

SARAH SLOYER

When Sarah Sloyer first discovered amigurumi, she became determined to teach herself how to crochet so she could make them! After lots of practice, she is finally designing and writing her own patterns, which she loves sharing with others. She has more patterns available for free download and purchase at: ***ravelry.com/stores/critterbeans.***

PATTERN NOTES

- The Chain Loop Stitch is a wild-looking stitch that is deceptively easy to learn! In this pattern, the sheep's body is worked evenly with minimal increasing and decreasing, so you can just focus on learning the chain loop technique. The stitch is a great way to add texture to your crocheted work: use it to create fun fringe on garments, durable pom-poms, homemade dish scrubbies, hair for a doll, or other amigurumi animals (works great for hedgehogs)! Once you've become comfortable with the technique, try experimenting with varying chain lengths and spacing.

Sleepy sheep

Crochet yourself this adorable and sleepy farm animal with chain loops

PATTERN

HEAD AND BODY

In col 1, make a magic ring.
Rnd 1 (RS): 6 dc into the magic ring. (6 sts)
Rnd 1: (1 dc in next st, 2 dc in next st) 3 times. (9 sts)
Rnd 2: (1 dc in next 2 sts, 2 dc in next st) 3 times. (12 sts)
Rnd 3: (1 dc in next 3 sts, 2 dc in next st) 3 times. (15 sts)
Rnd 4: (1 dc in next 4 sts, 2 dc in next st) 3 times. (18 sts)
Rnd 5: (1 dc in next 5 sts, 2 dc in next st) 3 times. (21 sts)
Rnd 6: (1 dc in next 6 sts, 2 dc in next st) 3 times. (24 sts)
Rnd 7: 1 dc in each st. (24 sts)
Rnd 8: 1 dc in next 5 sts, ch 8, re-insert hook into 5th dc (this is the st at the base of the ch 8) and ss to create ear, 1 dc in each of next 13 sts, ch 8, re-insert hook into the 13th st (this is the st at the base of the ch 8) and ss to create ear, 1 dc in next 5 sts, 1 dc in last st before marker, changing to col 2. (24 sts)
Embroider eyes, nose and mouth now.
Rnd 8: In col 2: (1 dc in next st, 2 dc in next st) 12 times. When you reach the ear loops from the previous round, make sure to push them forward and work behind them. (36 sts)
Rnd 9 (flo): (1 dc in next st, ch 4) 35 times, 1 dc in last st before marker but do not ch 4. (36 dc)
Rnd 10 (blo): In back loops leftover from previous rnd: 1 dc in each st. (36 sts)
Rnds 11-22: Rep Rnds 9-10 another 6 times. (36 sts)
Rnd 23 (flo): (1 dc in next st, ch 4) 35 times, 1 dc in last st before marker but do not ch 4. (36 sts)
Rnd 24: In back loops leftover from previous rnd: (1 dc in next 4 sts, dc2tog) 6 times. (30 sts)
Rnd 25 (flo): (1 dc in next st, ch 4) 29 times, 1 dc in last st before marker but do not ch 4. (30 sts)
Begin to stuff the sheep with fibrefill stuffing, continuing to stuff generously after completing the following rnds and until the end of the pattern.
Rnd 26: In back loops leftover from previous rnd: (1 dc in next 3 sts, dc2tog) 6 times. (24 sts)
Rnd 27 (flo): (1 dc in next st, ch 4) 23 times, 1 dc in last st before marker but do not ch 4. (24 sts)
Rnd 28: In back loops leftover from previous rnd: (dc in next 2 sts, dc2tog) 6 times. (18 sts)
Rnd 29 (flo): (1 dc in next st, ch 4) 17 times, 1 dc in last st before marker but do not ch 4. (18 sts)
Rnd 30: In back loops leftover from previous rnd: (1 dc in next st, dc2tog) 6 times. (12 sts)
Rnd 31 (flo): (1 dc in next st, ch 4) 11 times, 1 dc in last st before marker but do not ch 4. (12 sts)
Rnd 32: In back loops leftover from previous rnd: (dc2tog) 6 times. (6 sts)
Rnd 33 (flo): (1 dc in next st, ch 4) 5 times, 1 dc in last st before marker but do not ch 4. (6 sts)
Fasten off with a ss, leaving a tail.
Thread your tail onto a yarn needle and weave it through each of the 6 left over back loops, pulling tight to close the hole. Weave in tail.

LEGS (MAKE 4)

Using col 1, make a magic ring.
Rnd 1 (RS): 6 dc into the magic ring. (6 sts)
Rnds 2-5: 1 dc in each st. (6 sts)
Do not stuff. After completing Rnd 5, with your loop still on your hook, pinch the top of the leg flat and insert your hook through both sides of the leg and complete a dc. Repeat once more in the next stitch, through both sides, to close the top of the leg. Yo and pull through to fasten off, leaving a tail for sewing.

ASSEMBLY

To attach each leg, thread the leftover yarn tail onto a yarn needle. Push apart the chain loop stitches to reveal the body of the sheep underneath. Insert your needle under the dc stitches, back out and through the stitches on the top of the leg. Repeat a few times until secure, then weave in and trim ends.

DIFFICULTY

✂ ✂ ✂ ✂ ✂

WHAT YOU NEED

- 3.5mm hook (US E/4)
- Yarn needle
- Embroidery needle
- Black embroidery thread
- Pink embroidery thread
- Fibrefill stuffing
- You will need to use aran weight (worsted) yarn in two chosen colours. Here we have use Mondial Bio Soft in:

Colour 1: Off-white (100g)
Colour 2: Cream (100g)

MEASUREMENTS

10cm long and 9cm tall

SPECIAL STITCHES

Chain loop stitch: 1 dc in next st, ch 4.

Little dress-up doll

Little dress-up doll's head, body and legs are crocheted as one piece so there are fewer pieces to assemble

DIFFICULTY

WHAT YOU NEED

- Hook 3.25 mm (US D/3)
- 1 pair 6 mm safety eyes
- Yarn needle
- Fiberfill
- Black yarn
- Yarn In this project we have used Bernat Handicrafter Cotton. You will need to use worsted weight yarn, in your chosen colours.

Colour 1: Skin (2 balls of yarn)
Colour 3: Dress (1 ball of yarn)
Colour 4: Shoes (oddment)

MEASUREMENTS

22 cm tall,

HEAD, BODY AND LEGS

Using 3.25 mm hook and col 1, make a magic ring.
Rnd 1: 6 dc into the ring and pull it closed. (6 sts)
Rnd 2: 2 dc in each dc. (12 sts)
Rnd 3: (1 dc in next dc, 2 dc in next dc) 6 times. (18 sts)
Rnd 4: (1 dc in each of next 2 dc, 2 dc in next dc) 6 times. (24 sts)
Rnd 5: (1 dc in each of next 3 dc, 2 dc in next dc) 6 times. (30 sts)
Rnds 6-13: 1 dc in each dc. (8 rnds of 30 sts)
Rnd 14: (1 dc in each of next 3 dc, dc2tog in next 2 dc) 6 times. (24 sts)
Rnd 15: (1 dc in each of next 2 dc, dc2tog in next 2 dc) 6 times. (18 sts)

ASSEMBLE THE FACE

Insert 6mm safety eyes between rnd 9 and rnd 10 of the head and position them 3 stitches apart.
Embroider a mouth between the eyes on rnd 12 and rnd 13 using a yarn needle and black yarn.

Stuff the head firmly.

Rnd 16: (1 dc in next dc, dc2tog in next 2 dc) 6 times. (12 sts)
Rnd 17: (dc2tog in next 2 dc) 6 times. (6 sts)
Rnd 18: 2 dc in each dc. (12 sts)
Rnd 19: (1 dc in next dc, 2 dc in next dc) 6 times. (18 sts)
Rnd 20: (1 dc in each of next 2 dc, 2 dc in next dc) 6 times. (24 sts)
Rnds 21-32: 1 dc in each dc. (12 rnds of 24 sts)
Stuff the body firmly.

MAKE LEGS

Insert hook in the 12th dc of rnd 32 and join with ss to separate body into 2 sections for the legs (adjust the dc that you insert the hook into to make sure that the space where the body divides lines up with the eyes and mouth in the middle of the head).

Rnds 33-46: 1 dc in each dc around the 1st half of the body to form the 1st leg . (14 rnds of 12 sts).
Fasten off.

Insert crochet hook into a dc on the 2nd leg opening.

Rnds 1-14: 1 dc in each dc around the 2nd half of the body to form the 2nd leg. (14 rnds of 12 sts)
Stuff the legs firmly.

EARS (MAKE 2)

Using col 1, make a magic ring.
Work 6 dc into ring and pull it closed. Fasten off

ARMS (MAKE 2)

Using col 1, make a magic ring.
Rnd 1: 4 dc into ring and pull it closed. (4 sts)
Rnd 2: 2 dc in each dc. (8 sts)
Rnds 3-5: 1 dc in each dc. (3 rnds of 8 sts)
Rnd 6: (dc2tog in next 2 dc) 4 times. (4 sts)
Rnd 7: 2 dc in each dc. (8 sts)

DESIGNED BY

AMY KEMBER

Amy is a technical writer living in Ottawa, Canada. Her interest in crochet began when she discovered an amigurumi book in a used bookstore. After making a pig, she was instantly hooked. Since 2010, Amy has been designing and selling her own amigurumi patterns on Etsy. ***www.etsy.com/shop/AmysGurumis***

Rnds 8-19: 1 dc in each dc. (12 rnds of 8 sts)
Fasten off.

FEET (MAKE 2)

Using col 1, make a magic ring.
Rnd 1: 6 dc into ring and pull it closed. (6 sts)
Rnd 2: 2 dc in each dc. (12 sts)
Rnd 3: (2 dc in each of next 3 dc, 1 dc in each of next 3 dc) 2 times. (18 sts)
Rnd 4: 1 tr in each of next 10 dc, 1 dc in each of next 8 dc. (18 sts)
Rnd 5: (dc2tog in next 2 tr) 5 times, 1 dc in each of next 8 dc. (13 sts)
Fasten off.

HAIR (MAKE 2)

Using col 2, make a magic ring.
Rnd 1: 6 dc into ring and pull it closed. (6 sts)
Rnd 2: 2 dc in each dc. (12 sts)
Rnd 3: (1 dc in next dc, 2 dc in next dc) 6 times. (18 sts)
Rnd 4: (1 dc in each of next 2 dc, 2 dc in next dc) 6 times. (24 sts)
Rnd 5 (transition from rnds to rows): (1 dc in each of next 3 dc, 2 dc in next dc) 6 times, turn. (30 sts)
Row 6: ch 1, 1 dc in each of next 10 dc, 1 tr in each of next 10 dc, turn. (20 sts, leaving 10 dc unworked)
Row 7: ch 1, 1 tr in each of next 10 tr, 1 dc in each of next 10 dc, turn. (20 sts)
Row 8: ch 1, 1 dc in each of next 10 dc, 1 tr in each of next tr, turn. (20 sts)
Rows 9-11: ch 1, 1 dc in each st, turn. (3 Rows of 20 sts)

FORM CURLS

Row 12 (form curls): *ch 16, begin with 2nd ch from hook, 1 ss in each of next 15 ch, skip 1 dc, ss in next dc (one curl formed); repeat from * to last st, ch 16, begin with 2nd ch from hook, 1 ss in each of next 15 ch, ss in next dc. (10 curls made)
Fasten off leaving a long tail.

DRESS

Using col 3, ch 21.
Row 1: 1 dc into 2nd ch from hook, 1 dc in each ch to end, turn. (20 sts)
Row 2: ch 1, (1 dc in each of next 3 dc, 2 dc in next dc) 4 times, 1 dc in each of next 4 dc, turn. (24 sts)
Row 3: ch 1, (1 dc in each of next 4 dc, 2 dc in next dc) 4 times, 1 dc in each of next 4 dc, turn. (28 sts)
Row 4: ch 1, (1 dc in each of next 5 dc, 2 dc in next dc) 4 times, 1 dc in each of next 4 dc, turn. (32 sts)
Row 5: ch 1, (1 dc in each of next 6 dc, 2 dc in next dc) 4 times, 1 dc in each of next 4 dc, turn. (36 sts)
Row 6: ch 1, 1 dc in each dc, turn. (36 sts)

MAKE SLEEVES

Rnd 7 (transition from rows to rnds): ch 1, 1 dc in each of next 5 dc, 2 ch, skip 7 dc, join in 13th dc with ss, 1 dc in each of next 10 dc, 2 ch, skip 7 dc, join in 31st dc with ss, 1 dc in each of next 5 dc, join with ss and begin working in rnds. (24 sts)

NOTE: Do not count the slip sts from this rnd as sts in the following rnd)

Rnds 8-11: 1 dc in each dc. (4 rnds of 24 sts)
Rnd 12: (1 tr in next dc, 2 tr in next dc) 12 times. (36 sts)
Rnds 13-15: 1 tr in each tr. (3 rnds of 36 sts)
Rnd 16: 1 tr in each tr to last 3 sts, 1 htr, 1 dc, ss into last dc. (avoids jog at join.)
Fasten off.

ASSEMBLE THE DRESS

To finish off the dress, ch 3 and ss into the 1st st at the top of the dress (to form the button hole), then continue to ss along the opening of the dress until you reach the opposite side of the opening and
fasten off.
Using the other yarn end on the left side of the dress opening and a yarn needle, fasten a white button to the dress and weave in the ends.

SHOES (MAKE 2)

Using col 4, make a magic ring.
Rnd 1: 6 dc into ring and pull it closed. (6 sts)
Rnd 2: 2 dc in each dc. (12 sts)
Rnd 3: (2 dc in each of next 3 dc, 1 dc in each of next 3 dc) twice. (18 sts)
Rnd 4: 1 tr in each of next 10 dc, 1 dc in each of next 8 dc. (18 sts)
Rnd 5: (dc2tog in next 2 tr) 5 times, 1 dc in each of next 8 dc, do not fasten off. (13 sts)

MAKE SHOE STRAP

Ch 5, skip 4 dc, join in 5th dc with ss.
Fasten off.

FINISHING

Stuff the arms and feet.
Sew the hair to the head (stitch up the side of the head, along the front, down the other side of the head and then in between the hair piece and the curls along the back).
Sew the ears to the head.
Sew the arms to the body between rnd 19 and rnd 20 and position them 8 stitches apart in the front.
Sew the feet to the bottom of the legs.

Octopus hand puppet

Watch your child's imagination unfold under the sea, with this creative hand puppet

DIFFICULTY

WHAT YOU NEED

- 4mm hook (US G/6)
- Yarn needle
- Scissors
- For this project you will need worsted weight yarn in your chosen colours. Here we have used Lion Brand Vanna's Choice:

Colour 1: Dark Purple (A) (82g)
Colour 2: Light Purple (B) (6g)
Colour 1: White (oddments)
Colour 2: Black (oddments)

MEASUREMENTS

21cm (8in) long, 21cm (8in) wide

TENSION

7 sts across and 8 rnds down to measure approximately 5cm (2in)

SPECIAL STITCHES:

Invisible dc2tog; this is essentially a decrease, but worked in such a way as to make the continuous stitching smoother, and the decrease not as noticeable. Insert hook into front loop only of next st, then into front loop of 2nd st. Yoh and pull through 2 loops. Yoh and pull through last 2 loops.

PATTERN

BODY

Using col 1, make a magic ring.

Rnd 1 (RS): Work 6 dc into the ring. (6 sts)

Rnd 2: 2 dc in each st. (12 sts)

Rnd 3: (2 dc in next st, 1 dc in next st) 6 times. (18 sts)

Rnd 4: (2 dc in next st, 1 dc in next 2 sts) 6 times. (24 sts)

Rnd 5: (2 dc in next st, 1 dc in next 3 sts) 6 times. (30 sts)

Rnd 6: (2 dc in next 3 sts, 1 dc in next 12 sts) twice. (36 sts)

Rnds 7-9: 1 dc in each st. (36 sts)

Rnd 10: (Invdc2tog, 1 dc in next 16 sts) twice. (34 sts)

Rnd 11: 1 dc in each st. (34 sts)

Rnd 12: (Invdc2tog, 1 dc in next 15 sts) twice. (32 sts)

Rnd 13: 1 dc in each st. (32 sts)

Rnd 14: (Invdc2tog, 1 dc in next 14 sts) twice. (30 sts)

Rnd 15: (Invdc2tog, 1 dc in next 13 sts) twice. (28 sts)

Rnd 16: (Invdc2tog, 1 dc in next 12 sts) twice. (26 sts)

Rnd 17: (Invdc2tog, 1 dc in next 11 sts) twice. (24 sts)

Rnd 18: 1 dc in each st. (24 sts)

Rnd 19: (2 dc in next 3 sts, 1 dc in next 9 sts) twice. (30 sts)

Rnd 20: (Ch 4, sk next 4 sts, 1 dc in next 11 sts) twice. (30 sts)

Rnd 21: (1 dc into each of the 4 chs [using the back loop under the chs will create a neater look in the sts for sewing on the arms later], 1 dc in next 11 sts) twice. (30 sts)

(See picture above).

Rnds 22-34: 1 dc in each st. (30 sts)

Fasten off and weave in ends.

TENTACLES

(make 8 in col 1)

Two of the tentacles are for the finger holes on the puppet. The others will be sewn strategically around the body.

Using col 1, make a magic ring.

Rnd 1 (RS): Work 3 dc into the ring. (3 sts)

Rnd 2: 2 dc in next st, 1 dc in next 2 sts. (4 sts)

Rnd 3: 2 dc in next st, 1 dc in next 3 sts. (5 sts)

Rnd 4: 2 dc in next st, 1 dc in next 4 sts. (6 sts)

Rnd 5: 2 dc in next 2 sts, 1 dc in next st, invdc2tog, 1 dc in next st. (7 sts)

Rnd 6: 1 dc in next st, 2 dc in next st, 1 dc in next 5 sts. (8 sts)

Rnd 7: 1 dc in next 2 sts, 2 dc in next 2 sts, 1 dc in next 2 sts, invdc2tog. (9 sts)

DESIGNED BY

ERIN GREENE OF EKAYG

Erin is a work-at-home mum of four. She began making and designing toys to encourage creative play among her own children.
https://ekayg.com

Using the back loop under the chs will create a neater look in the sts for sewing on the arms later

Rnds 8-10: 1 dc in next 3 sts, 2 dc in next st, 1 dc in next 3 sts, invdc2tog. (9 sts)
Rnd 11: 1 dc in next 3 sts, 2 dc in next 2 sts, 1 dc in next 2 sts, invdc2tog. (10 sts)
Rnd 12: Invdc2tog, 1 dc in next 2 sts, 2 dc in next 2 sts, 1 dc in next 2 sts, invdc2tog. (10 sts)
Rnd 13: 1 dc in next 4 sts, 2 dc in next 2 sts, 1 dc in next 4 sts. (12 sts)
Rnds 14-16: 1 dc in each st. (12 sts)

Fasten off, leaving a long tail for sewing. Make and sew the undersides of the tentacles first, before sewing tentacles onto the body.

TENTACLE UNDERSIDE

(make 8 in col 2)
Using col 2, ch 4.
Row 1: 1 dc in 2nd ch from hook, and in each of the next 2 ch, turn. (3 sts)
Rows 2-4: Ch 1, 1 dc in each st, turn. (3 sts)
Row 5: Ch 1, sk 1st st, 1 dc in next 2 sts, turn. (2 sts)
Rows 6-10: Ch 1, 1 dc in each st, turn. (2 sts)
Row 11: Ch 1, sk 1st st, 1 dc in next st, turn. (1 st)
Row 12-13: Ch 1, 1 dc in st, turn. (1 st)

Fasten off, leaving a long tail for sewing. Sew onto the underside of all your tentacles. Be sure they are on the side that you want facing out! Sew 4 of them on with the tentacles curving left and 4 with the tentacles curving right.
Sew two of your tentacles into the arm holes of the puppet. Then sew one on each side, toward the bottom of the puppet, and four across the front. You can have some fun with these tentacles and sew them in different ways and different directions to give the octopus a unique look!

EYES

(make 2)
Using col 4, make a magic ring.
Rnd 1 (RS): Work 4 dc into the ring, join to 1st st with ss. (4 sts)

Change to col 2.
Rnd 2: 2 dc into same st as joining, 2 dc in each remaining st around, join to 1st st with ss. (8 sts)

Change to col 3.
Rnd 3: 2 dc into same st as joining, 1 dc in next st, (2 dc in next st, 1 dc in next st) 3 times, join to 1st st with ss. (12 sts)
Rnd 4: Sk joining st, 2 htr in next st, 1 dc in next 2 sts, (1 htr, 1 tr) in next st, 1 tr in next st, 1 htr in next st, (1 htr, 1 dc) into next st, 1 dc in next 2 sts, 2 htr in next st, ss in next st, but do not join to the first st.

Fasten off, leaving a long tail for sewing. Sew onto the face as pictured, low on the head.

Have fun with the tentacles and sew them in different ways and different directions

PATTERN NOTES

• This pattern is worked from the top down, in the round, with no joining. The eyes and tentacles are made separately and sewn on. Pictures shown here can give more details into the process. The finished puppet is one size, fitting child through adult, but if you wish to make it smaller for a smaller child to play with, simply tighten the gauge or go down a hook size.

Depending on how you've sewn on the tentacles, the octopus will have a unique look

Ready for some under-the-sea fun

DESIGNED BY

AMY KEMBER

Amy is a technical writer living in Ottawa, Canada. Her interest in crochet began when she discovered an amigurumi book in a used bookstore. After making a pig, she was instantly hooked. Since 2010, Amy has been designing and selling her own amigurumi patterns on Etsy. ***www.etsy.com/shop/AmysGurumis/***

Giant mouse

This jumbo-sized amigurumi mouse is bigger than the mice you'll find in mouse holes, but also much cuddlier!

DIFFICULTY

✂ ✂ ✂ ✂ ✂

WHAT YOU NEED

- Yarn needle
- Fibrefill
- 1 pair 9mm safety eyes
- Pink & grey felt
- Small pink button
- Hot glue gun
- In this project we have used Bernat Handicrafter Cotton. You will need to use DK weight yarn in your chosen colours.

Colour: Body (3 balls)

HOOK

3.75mm (US F/5)

MEASUREMENTS

33cm tall

PATTERN

GIANT MOUSE

HEAD

Using 3.75mm hook, make a magic ring.

Rnd 1: 6 dc into ring and pull it closed. (6 sts)
Rnd 2: 2 dc in each dc. (12 sts)
Rnd 3: (1 dc in next dc, 2 dc in the next dc) 6 times. (18 sts)
Rnd 4: (1 dc in each of next 2 dc, 2 dc in next dc) 6 times. (24 sts)
Rnd 5: (1 dc in each of next 3 dc, 2 dc in next dc) 6 times. (30 sts)
Rnd 6: (1 dc in each of next 4 dc, 2 dc in next dc) 6 times. (36 sts)
Rnd 7: (1 dc in each of next 5 dc, 2 dc in next dc) 6 times. (42 sts)
Rnds 8-12: 1 dc in each dc. (5 rnds of 42 sts)
Rnd 13: ss in each dc. (42 sts)
Rnd 14: (1 dc in each of next 6 dc, 2 dc in next dc) 6 times. (48 sts)
Rnd 15: (1 dc in each of next 7 dc, 2 dc in next dc) 6 times. (54 sts)
Rnd 16: (1 dc in each of next 8 dc, 2 dc in next dc) 6 times. (60 sts)
Rnds 17-21: 1 dc in each dc. (5 rnds of 60 sts)
Rnd 22: (1 dc in each of next 8 dc, dc2tog over next 2 sts) 6 times. (54 sts)
Rnd 23: (1 dc in each of next 7 dc, dc2tog over next 2 sts) 6 times. (48 sts)
Rnd 24: (1 dc in each of next 6 dc, dc2tog over next 2 sts) 6 times. (42 sts)
Rnd 25: (1 dc in each of next 5 dc, dc2tog over next 2 sts) 6 times. (36 sts)
Rnd 26: (1 dc in each of next 4 dc, dc2tog over next 2 sts) 6 times. (30 sts)
Rnd 27: (1 dc in each of next 3 dc, dc2tog over next 2 sts) 6 times. (24 sts)
Fasten off.

BODY

MAKE A MAGIC RING

Rnd 1: 6 dc into ring and pull it closed. (6 sts)
Rnd 2: 2 dc in each dc. (12 sts)
Rnd 3: (1 dc in next dc, 2 dc in next dc) 6 times. (18 sts)
Rnd 4: (1 dc in each of next 2 dc, 2 dc in next dc) 6 times. (24 sts)
Rnd 5: (1 dc in each of next 3 dc, 2 dc in next dc) 6 times. (30 sts)
Rnd 6: (1 dc in each of next 4 dc, 2 dc in next dc) 6 times. (36 sts)
Rnd 7: (1 dc in each of next 5 dc, 2 dc in next dc) 6 times. (42 sts)
Rnd 8: (1 dc in each of next 6 dc, 2 dc in next dc) 6 times. (48 sts)
Rnd 9: (1 dc in each of next 7 dc, 2 dc in next dc) 6 times. (54 sts)
Rnds 10-12: 1 dc in each dc. (3 rnds of 54 sts)
Rnd 13: (1 dc in each of next 7 dc, dc2tog over next 2 sts) 6 times. (48 sts)
Rnds 14-17: dc in each dc. (4 rnds of 48 sts)
Rnd 18: (1 dc in each of next 6 dc, dc2tog over next 2 sts) 6 times. (42 sts)
Rnds 19-20: 1 dc in each dc. (2 rnds of 42 sts)
Rnd 21: (1 dc in each of next 5 dc, dc2tog over next 2 sts) 6 times.(36 sts)
Rnd 22: (1 dc in each of next 4 dc, dc2tog over next 2 sts) 6 times. (30 sts)
Rnds 23-25: 1 dc in each dc. (3 rnds of 30 sts)
Fasten off

EARS (MAKE 2)

MAKE A MAGIC RING

Rnd 1: 6 dc into ring and pull it closed. (6 sts)
Rnd 2: 2 dc in each dc. (12 sts)
Rnd 3: (1 dc in next dc, 2 dc in next dc) 6 times. (18 sts)
Rnd 4: (1 dc in each of the next 2 dc, 2 dc in next dc) 6 times. (24 sts)
Rnds 5-8: 1 dc in each dc. (4 rnds of 24 sts)
Rnd 9: (1 dc in each of next 2 dc, dc2tog over next 2 sts) 6 times. (18 sts)
Rnd 10: (1 dc in next dc, dc2tog over next 2 sts) 6 times. (12 sts)
Fasten off.

ARMS (MAKE 2)

MAKE A MAGIC RING

Rnd 1: 6 dc into ring and pull it closed. (6 sts)
Rnd 2: 2 dc in each dc. (12 sts)
Rnd 3: (1 dc in next dc, 2 dc in next dc) 6 times. (18 sts)
Rnds 4-5: 1 dc in each dc. (2 rnds of 18 sts)
Rnd 6: (1 dc in next dc, dc2tog over next 2 sts) 6 times. (12 sts)

Rnds 7-12: 1 dc in each cc. (6 rnds of 12 sts)
Rnd 13: (dc2tog over next 2 sts) 6 times. (6 sts)
Fasten off.

LEGS (MAKE 2) MAKE A MAGIC RING

Rnd 1: 6 dc into ring and pull it closed. (6 sts)
Rnd 2: 2 dc in each dc. (12 sts)
Rnd 3: (1 dc in next dc, 2 dc in next dc) 6 times. (18 sts)
Rnd 4: (1 dc in each of next 2 dc, 2 dc in next dc) 6 times. (24 sts)
Rnds 5-7: 1 dc in each dc. (3 rnds of 24 sts)
Rnd 8: (1 dc in each of next 2 dc, dc2tog over next 2 sts) 6 times. (18 sts)
Rnd 9: (1 dc in next dc, dc2tog over next 2 sts) 6 times. (12 sts)
Rnds 10-15: 1 dc in each dc. (6 rnds of 12 sts)
Fasten off.

TAIL

Ch 31.
1 dc into 2nd ch from hook, 1 dc into each ch to end. (30 sts)
Fasten off.

ASSEMBLE THE FACE

Insert 9mm safety eyes between rnd 13 and rnd 14 of the head and position them approx 8 sts apart. Stuff the head firmly.
Cut out a grey felt mouth using the template provided. Sew a pink button nose in the centre of the mouth using a yarn needle and yarn. Referring to the photograph, position the mouth and nose between the eyes. Glue the mouth and nose to mouse's face using a hot glue gun.

ASSEMBLE THE BODY

Sew the body to the head – note there is one extra decrease rnd on the head than on the body so the last rnd of the body (rnd 26) should be sewn around the second last rnd on the head (rnd 27).
Sew the arms to the body between rnd 25 and rnd 26 positioning them 6 stitches apart on the front.
Sew the legs to the body between rnd 8 and rnd 9 positioning them 2 stitches apart in the front.
Cut out two pink felt fears using the template provided. Glue felt to each crocheted ear using a hot glue gun. Sew the ears to the head between rnd 10 and rnd 14.
Sew the tail to the body between rnd 10 and rnd 11.

"Children will have so much fun playing with this adorable mouse"

Football captain

Create a miniature footballer with trophy and football accessories – even change colours to match a team

DIFFICULTY

✂ ✂ ✂ ✂ ✂

WHAT YOU NEED

- Yarn needle
- 2 mm (US B/1) Hook
- Fibrefill
- Black & red thread
- In this project we have used King Cole 4 ply Bamboo.
- You will need to use 4 ply weight yarn, in your chosen colours.
  - Colour 1: Skin (1 ball)
  - Colour 2: Boot soles (oddment)
  - Colour 3: Boots (oddment)
  - Colour 4: White(1 ball)
  - Colour 5: Hair (oddment)
  - Colour 6: Shirt (1 ball)
  - Colour 7: Black (oddment)
  - Colour 8: Trophy (oddment)

MEASUREMENTS

Approx 20cm tall, depending on hook and yarn size used

PATTERN
FOOTBALL CAPTAIN

HEAD

Using 2mm hook and col 1, make a magic ring.

Rnd 1: 6 dc into the ring and pull it closed. (6 sts)

Rnd 2: 2 dc in each dc. (12 sts)

Rnd 3: (1 dc in next dc, 2 dc in next dc) 6 times. (18 sts)

Rnd 4: (1 dc in each of next 2 dc, 2 dc in next dc) 6 times. (24 sts)

Rnd 5: (1 dc in each of next 3 dc, 2 dc in next dc) 6 times. (30 sts)

Rnds 6-13: 1 dc in each dc. (8 rnds of 30 sts)

Rnd 14: (1 dc in each of next 3 dc, dc2tog in next 2 dc) 6 times. (24 sts)

Rnd 15: (1 dc in each of next 2 dc, dc2tog in next 2 dc) 6 times. (18 sts)

Lightly stuff.

Rnd 16: (1 dc in next dc, dc2tog in next 2 dc) 6 times. (12 sts)

Rnd 17: (1 dc in next 2 dc, dc2tog in next 2 dc) 3 times. (9 sts)

Rnd 18: 1 dc in each dc. (9 sts)

Fasten off.

BOOTS, SOCKS AND LEGS

FIRST LEG

Using col 2, ch 5.

Rnd 1: 2 dc into 2nd ch from hook, 1 dc in each of next ch 2, 4 dc in next ch, rotate work to cont along bottom of ch, 1 dc in each of next ch 2, 4 dc in next ch. (14 sts)

Rnd 2: 2 dc in next dc, 1 dc in each of next 3 dc, 2 htr in each of next 4 dc, 1 dc in each of next 3 dc, 2 dc in each of next 3 dc. (22 sts)

NOTE: You should now be at the heel of the foot.

Change to col 3.

Rnd 3 (flo): 1 dc in each st. (22 sts)

Rnd 4: 1 dc in each of next 9 dc, (dc2tog in next 2 dc) twice, 1 dc in each of next 9 dc. (20 sts)

Rnd 5: 1 dc in each of next 6 dc, 1 htr in each of next 8 htr, 1 dc in each of next 6 dc. (20 sts)

Rnd 6: 1 dc in each of next 6 dc, (dc2tog in next 2 htr) 4 times, 1 dc in each of next 6 dc. (16 sts)

Change to col 4.

Rnd 7 (flo): 1 dc in each of next 5 dc, (dc2tog in next 2 dc) 3 times, 1 dc in each of next 5 dc. (13 sts)

Rnd 8: 1 dc in each of next 4 dc, (dc2tog in next 2 dc) twice, 1 dc in each of next 5 dc. (11 sts)

Stuff the foot, continue to leg.

Rnd 9: 1 dc in each of next 4 dc, dc2tog in next 2 dc, 1 dc in each of next 5 dc. (10 sts)

Rnd 10: 1 dc in each of next 3 dc, (dc2tog in next 2 dc) twice, 1 dc in each of next 3 dc. (8 sts)

Rnd 11-14 (flo): 1 dc in each dc. (4 rnds of 8 sts)

Rnd 15 (flo): 2 dc in next dc, 1 dc in each of next 6 dc, 2 dc in next dc. (10 sts)

Rnds 16-18 (flo): 1 dc in each dc. (3 rnds of 10 sts)

Change to col 1.

Rnd 19 (flo): dc2tog in next 2 dc, 1 dc in each of next 3 dc, 2 dc in each of next 2 dc, 1 dc in each of next 3 dc. (11 sts)

Rnd 20: 1 dc in each of next 5 dc, 1 htr in next 4 dc, 1 dc in each of next 2 dc. (11 sts)

Stuff lower leg.

Rnd 21: 1 dc in each st. (11 sts)

Rnd 22: 1 dc in each of next 5 dc, 2 dc in each of next dc, 1 dc in each of next 5 dc. (12 sts)

DESIGNED BY

KATRINA EVA

A designer of patterns featuring small dolls and animals, Katrina enjoys creating lifelike miniatures with character and style. She has developed a special interest in custom-made crocheted pets from photos. Her greyhounds and whippets have proved especially popular and have been ordered by customers in the UK and Europe.
www.heartfelt2inspire.co.uk
www.etsy.com/uk/shop/KatyJaneCreations

Rnd 23: (2 dc in next dc, 1 dc in each of next 5 dc) twice. (14 sts)
Rnds 24-33: 1 dc in each dc. (10 rnds of 14 sts)
Fasten off, adding more stuffing if needed, twist leg a little until foot and knee are facing in same direction.

SECOND LEG

Work rnds 1-33 as for first leg but do not fasten off.
Stuff both legs, hold first leg next to second in position making sure knees are facing the same way, feet towards you. Make sure yarn is on far right side of the doll by your right hand, still on second leg.

JOIN LEGS

With legs held side-by-side and squeezed flat along tops, ch 1, 1 dc in each dc straight across first leg through 2 thicknesses, then cont across other leg to join as one piece, turn. (14st - 7 dc for each leg)
Rnd 34: ch 1, 1 dc in each of next 14 dc along the back loops, then turn and cont working 1 dc in each of next 14 dc in front loops. (28 sts)
Rnd 35: 1 dc in each dc. (28 sts)
Rnd 36: 1 dc in each of next 2 dc, 2 dc in next dc, (1 dc in next dc, 2 dc in next dc) 3 times, 1 dc in each of next 19 dc. (32 sts)
Rnd 37: (dc2tog in next 2 dc, 1 dc in each of next 2 dc) 3 times, dc2tog in next 2 dc, 1 dec in each of next 18 dc. (28 sts)
Rnd 38: (dc2tog in next 2 dc, 1 dc in each of next 5 dc) 3 times, dc2tog in next 2 dc, 1 dc in each of next 5 dc. (24 sts)
Rnd 39 (blo): 1 dc in each dc. (24 sts)
Rnd 40: 1 dc in each dc. (24 sts)
Rnd 41: (2 dc in next dc, 1 dc in each of next 2 dc) 3 times, 2 dc in next dc, 1 dc in next 14 dc. (28 sts)
Rnds 42-49: 1 dc in each dc. (8 rnds of 28 sts)
Rnd 50: 1 dc in each of next 5 dc, dc2tog in next 2 dc, 1 dc in each of next 2 dc, (dc2tog in next 2 dc) twice, 1 dc in each of next 2 dc, dc2tog in next 2 dc, 1 dc in each of next 11 dc. (24 sts)
Rnd 51: (1 dc in each of next 4 dc, dc2tog in next 2 dc) 4 times. (20 sts)
Rnd 52: (1 dc in each of next 3 dc, dc2tog in next 2 dc) 4 times. (16 sts)
Rnd 53: (dc2tog in next 2 dc) 3 times, 1 dc in each of next 4 dc, (dc2tog in next 2 dc) 3 times. (10 sts)
Stuff body.
Rnd 54: (1 dc in each of next 3 dc, dc2tog in next 2 dc) twice. (8 sts)
Rnds 55-57: 1 dc in each dc. (3 rnds of 8 sts)
Fasten off, adding a little more stuffing into the neck.
Attach head to body, catching alternate stitches from head and neck. Using col 2, add laces to the football boots.

ARMS (MAKE 2)

Using col 1, make a magic ring leaving 7cm tail (later to become thumb).
Rnd 1: 4 dc into the ring and pull it closed. (4 sts)
Rnd 2: 2 dc in each of next 4 dc. (8 sts)
Rnds 3-4: 1 dc in each dc. (2 rnds of 8 sts)
Rnd 5: dc2tog in next 2 dc, 1 dc in each of next 6 dc. (7 sts)
Rnd 6: dc2tog in next 2 dc, 1 dc in each of next 5 dc. (6 sts)
Rnds 7-14: 1 dc in each dc. (8 rnds of 6 sts)
Rnd 15: dc2tog in next 2 dc, 1 dc in each of next 2 dc, 2 dc in next dc, 1 dc

in next dc. (6 sts)
Rnd 16: 1 dc in each of next 3 dc, 1 htr in each of next 3 dc.
Rnd 17: 1 dc in next dc, 2 dc in next dc, 1 dc in each of next 4 sts. (7 sts)
Rnds 18-25: 1 dc in each dc. (8 rnds of 7 sts)
Stuff arms lightly.
Insert hook near thumb position on hand, out through end of hand and pull back tail.
Insert hook into exact thumb position hole and pull tail through to make a loop, ch 2, fasten off.
Pull end of tail back through same hole leaving thumb sticking out and use hook to hide rest of tail inside arm.
Sew arms to body.

WIG CAP, HAIR AND FACE

Using col 5, work rnds 1-5 as for head. (30 sts)
Rnd 6: (1 dc in each of next 4 dc, 2 dc in next dc) 6 times. (36 sts)
Rnd 7: (1 dc in each of next 5 dc, 2 dc in next dc) 6 times. (42 sts)
Rnd 8: (1 dc in each of next 6 dc, 2 dc in next dc) 6 times. (48 sts)
Rnd 9: (1 dc in each of next 6 dc, dc2tog in next 2 dc) 6 times. (42 sts)
Rnds 10-11: 1 dc in each dc. (2 rnds of 42 sts)

FRONT HAIR/FRINGE

Rnd 12 (transition to rows): 1 dc in each of next 6 dc, turn. (6 sts)
Row 13: ch 1, 1 dc in each dc. (6 sts)
Fasten off wig cap leaving long tail for sewing.
Sew cap at a slight angle to the back/top of the head, catching stitches around the edges of the cap, but not too tight as to distort the head shape.

Embroider a face onto your doll. For the nose, choose 4 sts in the centre of the face and slip stitch around them, pulling thread through with a needle.

Stitch a few strands of wool from the edge of the cap towards back of head to give a hairstyle as in the picture, or use your imagination to copy the hairstyle of your chosen football character.
For a short style, attach individual cut strands at random by inserting the hook under a dc, doubling a cut strand and catching a loop, pulling it part-way through and then insert the two loose ends through the loop, pulling tight.
Weave these randomly into the cap until you it's covered. You can then cut and style the hair, but not too short otherwise the strands might pull through.
Our doll is sporting a Gareth Bale hairstyle.

SHORTS

With doll held upside down and facing away from you, join with col 4 at back of doll's waist with ss to a loop from rnd 40.
Rnds 1-2: 1 dc in each loop around waist. (24 sts)
Rnd 3: (1 dc in each of next 2 dc, 2 dc in next dc) 8 times. (32 sts)
Rnd 4: (1 dc in each of next 3 dc, 2 dc in next dc) 8 times. (40 sts)
Rnd 5-6: 1 dc in each dc. (2 rnds of 40 sts)

FIRST LEG

Skip 20 sts. Ss between the legs into 21st st from previous rnd. This divides work into 2 and you will now work each leg of the shorts separately.
Rnd 7: ch 3, 1 tr into ss just made, 1 tr in each of next 19 dc. (20 sts)
Rnd 8: ch 3, 1 tr in each tr, join with ss. (20 sts)
Fasten off. Weave end to hide inside leg.

SECOND LEG

With doll still held upside down and facing away from you, rejoin col 4 with ss in st 40 from rnd 6 (at inside leg).
Rnd 7: ch 3, 1 tr in each of next 19 dc, 1 tr in joining ss from 1st leg. (20 sts)
Rnd 8: ch 3, 1 tr in each of next 20 tr, join with ss. (20 sts)
Fasten off and weave end inside leg.

SHIRT

Using col 7, ch 17.
Row 1: 2 htr in 3rd ch from hook and then 2 htr in each ch to end, turn. (30 sts)
Row 2 (make armholes): ch 2, 1 htr in next 5 htr, ch 5, skip next 5 htr, 1 htr in each of next 10 htr, ch 5, skip next 5 htr, 1 htr in each of next 5 htr, turn. (30 sts)
Row 3: ch 2, 1 htr in each of next 5 htr, 5 htr in ch-sp, 1 htr in each of next 10 htr, 5 htr in ch-sp, 1 htr in each of next 5 dc, turn. (30 sts)
Row 4-7: ch 2, 1 htr in each of next 30 htr, turn. (4 rnds of 30 sts)
Row 8: ch 2, (1 htr in each of next 9 htr, 2 htr in next htr) twice, 1 htr in each of next 10 htr, turn. (32 sts)
Row 9: ch 2, (1 htr in each of next 10 htr, 2 htr in next htr) twice, 10 htr, turn. (34 sts)
Row 10: ch 2, 1 htr in each htr. (34 sts)
Fasten off leaving long

Horace the monster

Make a cute litte monster with multiple eyes, for children of all ages to enjoy

DIFFICULTY

✂ ✂ ✂ ✂ ✂

WHAT YOU NEED

- 2.75mm hook (US C/2)
- Safety eyes: five x 18mm, six x 9mm, four x 12mm
- Fiberfill stuffing
- White felt for the tooth
- Glue to attach the tooth
- You will need an Aran weight yarn. We have used Rosario 4: Catitano in:

Colour 1: White (50g)
Colour 2: Blue (50g)
Colour 3: Dark blue (50g)
Colour 4: Grey (50g)
Colour 5: Yellow (50g)

MEASUREMENTS

28cm tall, while standing, and 12.75cm wide

SPECIAL STITCHES:

Surface crochet: crocheting directly into the body of the amigurumi.

3 dtr popcorn stitch: work a dtr to the last yarn over (2 loop left on hook), stop and create two more incomplete dtr sts. You should have 4 loops on your hook. yo and pull through all loops.

2 tr popcorn stitch: work a tr to the last yarn over (2 loops left on hook), stop and create one more incomplete trst. You should have 3 loops on your hook. yo and pull through all loops.

PATTERN

Note: Be aware that when you work with the wrong side out the front and back loops of a stitch will be reversed. When you see instructions written as "flo (blo)" in this pattern, you will work what is before the brackets if you are crocheting with the right side out, and you will work what is in the brackets if you are working with the wrong side facing out.

SMALL EYE (MAKE 6)

Using 2.75mm hook and col 1, make a magic ring.
Rnd 1 (RS): 5 dc into the magic ring. (5 sts)
Place your 9mm safety eye in the middle of the magic ring and pull the ring tight around the post. After rnd 2, fix the back of the safety eye in place.
Rnd 2: 2 dc in each st. (10 sts)
Change to col 2.
Rnds 3-5: 1 dc in each st. (10 sts)
Stuff with fiberfill and continue stuffing as you go.
Rnd 6: (dc2tog) 5 times. (5 sts)
Fasten off, leaving a long tail for sewing. Using your yarn needle, weave the yarn tail through the front loop of each remaining stitch and pull it tight to close. Do not cut yarn.
For the rim, have the white of the small eye facing you, think of the eye as a clock, and attach col 2 at the 12 o'clock position between rnds 2-3.

Note: If you attach the yarn at 6 o'clock the eye rim will be reversed and incorrect.

Rnd 1 (RS): ch 1 (not counted as a st here and throughout), 1 dc in next 10 sts, ss into first dc. (10 sts)
Rnd 2: ch 1, (2 dc in next st, 1 dc in next 4 sts) twice, ss into first dc. (12 sts) (See Fig. 2)
Fasten off and darn in all ends.

MEDIUM EYE (MAKE 4)

Using 2.75mm hook and col 1, make a magic ring.
Rnd 1 (RS): 5 dc into the magic ring. (5 sts)
Place your 12mm safety eye in the middle of the magic ring and pull the ring tight around the post. After rnd 2, fix the back of the safety eye in place.

DESIGNED BY

MEVLINN GUSICK

Mevlinn is a college graduate with a BFA in Fine Arts Painting. Her interest in knitting and crochet began when her aunt suggested she try knitting. It peaked her curiosity and here she is today, crocheting amigurumi whenever she gets the chance and giving them to those she loves.

www.mevvsan.com

Rnd 2: 2 dc in each st. (10 sts)
Rnd 3: (2 dc in next st, 1 dc in next st) 5 times. (15 sts)
Change to col 2.
Rnds 4-6: 1 dc in each st. (15 sts)
Rnd 7: (dc2tog, 1 dc in next st) 5 times. (10 sts)
Stuff with fiberfill and continue stuffing as you go.
Rnd 8: (dc2tog) 5 times. (5 sts)
Fasten off, leaving a long tail for sewing. Using your yarn needle, weave the yarn tail through the front loop of each remaining stitch and pull it tight to close. Leave the remaining yarn tail so you can use it to sew the eye to the body later.
Complete the rim of the eye as you did for the small eye.
Rnd 1 (RS): ch 1 (not counted as a st here and throughout), 1 dc in next 15 sts, ss into first dc. (15 sts)
Rnd 2: ch 1, (2 dc in next st, 1 dc in next 4 sts) 3 times, ss into first st. (18 sts) (See Fig. 2)
Fasten off and weave in all yarn ends.

LARGE EYE (MAKE 5)

Using 2.75mm hook and col 1, make a magic ring.
Rnd 1 (RS): 5 dc into the magic ring. (5 sts)
Place your 18mm safety eye in the middle of the magic ring and pull the ring tight around the post. After rnd 2, fix the back of the safety eye in place.
Rnd 2: 2 dc in each st. (10 sts)
Rnd 3: (2 dc in next st, 1 dc in next st) 5 times. (15 sts)
Rnd 4: (2 dc in next st, 1 dc in next 2 sts) 5 times. (20 sts)
Change to col 2.
Rnds 5-7: 1 dc in each st. (20 sts)
Rnd 8: (dc2tog, 1 dc in next 2 sts) 5 times. (15 sts)
Stuff with fiberfill and continue stuffing as you go.
Rnd 9: (dc2tog, 1 dc in next st) 5 times. (10 sts)
Rnd 10: (dc2tog) 5 times. (5 sts)
Fasten off, leaving a long tail for sewing. Using your yarn needle, weave the yarn tail through the front loop of each remaining stitch and pull it tight to close. Leave the remaining yarn tail so you can use it to sew the eye to the body later.
Complete the rim of the eye as you did for the small eye.
Rnd 1 (RS): ch 1 (not counted as a st here and throughout), 1 dc in next 20 sts, ss into first dc. (20 sts)
Rnd 2: ch 1, (2 dc in next st, 1 dc in next 4 sts) 4 times, ss into first dc. (24 sts) (See Fig. 2)
Fasten off and darn in all ends.

BODY

Using 2.75mm hook and col 2, make a magic ring.
Rnd 1 (RS): 8 dc into the magic ring. (8 sts)
Rnd 2: 2 dc in each st. (16 sts)
Rnd 3: (2 dc in next st, 1 dc in next st) 8 times. (24 sts)
Rnd 4: (2 dc in next st, 1 dc in next 2 sts) 8 times. (32 sts)
Rnd 5: (2 dc in next st, 1 dc in next 3 sts) 8 times. (40 sts)
Rnd 6: (2 dc in next st, 1 dc in next 4 sts) 8 times. (48 sts)
Rnd 7: 1 dc in each st. (48 sts)
Rnd 8: (2 dc in next st, 1 dc in next 5 sts) 8 times. (56 sts)
Rnds 9-12: 1 dc in each st. (56 sts)
Rnd 13: (dc2tog, 1 dc in next 12 sts) 4 times. (52 sts)
Rnd 14: 1 dc in each st. (52 sts)
Rnd 15: (dc2tog, 1 dc in next 11 sts) 4 times (48 sts)
Rnd 16: 1 dc in each st. (48 sts)
Rnd 17: (dc2tog, 1 dc in next 10 sts) 4 times. (44 sts)
Rnd 18: 1 dc in each st. (44 sts)
Rnd 19: (dc2tog, 1 dc in next 9 sts) 4 times. (40 sts)
Rnd 20: 1 dc in each st. (40 sts)

Rnd 21: (dc2tog, 1 dc in next 8 sts) 4 times. (36 sts)
Stuff with fiberfill and continue stuffing as you go.
Rnd 22 BLO (FLO): 1dc in next 9 sts, 1 dc in both loops of remaining 27 sts. (36 sts)
Rnd 23: 1 dc in each st. (36 sts)
Rnd 24: (dc2tog, 1 dc in next 7 sts) 4 times. (32 sts)
Rnds 25-26: 1 dc in each st. (32 sts)
Rnd 27: (dc2tog, 1 dc in next 6 sts) 4 times. (28 sts)
Rnds 28-29: 1 dc in each st. (28 sts)
Rnd 30: (dc2tog, 1 dc in next 5 sts) 4 times. (24 sts)
Rnds 31-32: 1 dc in each st. (24 sts)
Rnd 33: (dc2tog, 1 dc in next 4 sts) 4 times. (20 sts)
Rnds 34-35: 1 dc in each st. (20 sts)
Rnd 36: (dc2tog, 1 dc in next 2 sts) 5 times. (15 sts)
Rnd 37: (dc2tog, 1 dc in next st) 5 times. (10 sts)
Rnd 38: (dc2tog) 5 times. (5 sts)
Fasten off, leaving a tail for sewing. Using your yarn needle, weave the yarn tail through the front loop of each remaining stitch and pull it tight to close.

BODY LINES

With the back of the body facing you, attach col 3 between rnds 17-16. (Fig 3) Begin to surface crochet by slip stitching evenly around the body until you reach the point you started from. ss into first st and fasten off. Weave in all ends.
Repeat this for the remaining 4 lines starting with col 4 for between rnds 16-15, col 5 for rnds 15-14, col 4 for rnds 14-13 and col 3 for rnds 13-12.

MOUTH

Using 2.75mm hook and col 2, ss into the first unworked loop from rnd 22 of the body on the far right side. 1 dc into the same st, 1 htr in each st until the second to last st, 1 dc in next st, ss in the last st. Fasten off, weave in all yarn ends.

TOOTH

Cut a small triangle out of white felt and glue it with some craft or fabric glue so the lip of the mouth overlaps it.

FOOT AND LEG (MAKE 2)

Using 2.75m hook and col 2, make a magic ring.
Rnd 1 (RS): 6 dc into the magic ring. (6 sts)
Rnd 2: 2 dc in each st. (12 sts)
Rnd 3: (2 dc in next st, 1 dc in next st) 6 times. (18 sts)
Rnd 4: (3 dtr popcorn st in next st, 1 dc in next st) 4 times (See Fig. 4), dc in next 10 sts. (18 sts)
Rnd 5: 1 dc in each st. (18 sts)
Rnd 6: (dc2tog, 1 dc in next st) 6 times. (12 sts)
Rnd 7: (dc2tog, 1 dc in next st) 4 times. (8 sts)
Stuff with fiberfill and continue stuffing as you go.
Rnds 8-15: 1 dc in each st. (8 sts)
Fasten off, leaving a long tail for sewing. Sew the feet to the bottom of the body on either sides of the body's magic ring.

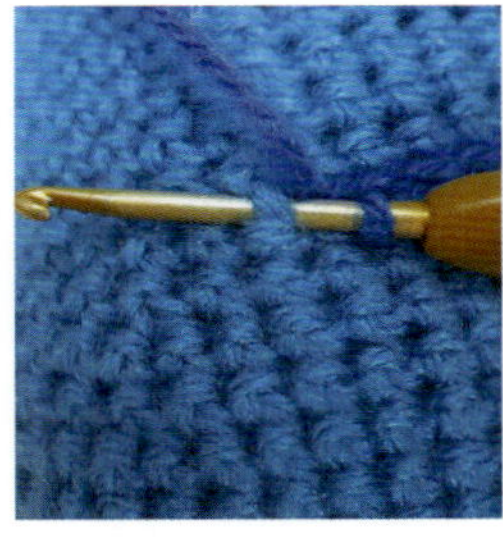

HAND AND ARM (MAKE 2)

Using 2.75mm hook and col 2, make a magic ring.
Rnd 1 (RS): 6 dc into the magic ring. (6 sts)
Rnd 2: 2 dc in each st. (12 sts)
Rnd 3: (2 dc in next st, 1 dc in next st) 6 times. (18 sts)
Rnds 4-5: 1 dc in each st. (18 sts)
Rnd 6: (dc2tog, 1 dc in next st) 6 times. (12 sts)
Rnd 7: (dc2tog) 6 times. (6 sts)
Stuff with fiberfill and continue stuffing as you go.
Rnds 8-17: 1 dc in each st. (6 sts)
Fasten off, leaving a long tail for sewing. Sew the arms onto the body between the mouth and the top dark blue body line.

FINGERS

Using 2.75mm hook and col 2, attach your yarn onto one of the stitches on either side of the hand's magic ring. ch 2, work a 2 tr popcorn st in the same space. Turn your hook, and your work, so that you can dc back into the same stitch you started. Fasten off and weave in all yarn ends. Repeat this 3 more times.

ATTACHING THE EYES

With the yarn tail left over from making each eye you can now sew the eyes onto the head. Sew the entire back of the eye onto the body in a circle as this will be more secure. As you add more eyes they will begin to touch and you can sew the eye the ones adjacent to it, this will make the toy safer for young children. We recommend trying to keep two eyes the same size from being next to each other for a better final effect.

Little bunny

Use up leftover yarn to crochet a little bunny with fun, striped legs and a cute removable t-shirt!

DIFFICULTY

✂ ✂ ✂ ✂ ✂

WHAT YOU NEED

- 1 pair 9mm safety eyes
- Yarn needle
- Fiberfill
- Pink and white felt
- Hot glue gun
- Small pom-pom for tail

In this project we have used Bernat Handicrafter Cotton.

You will need to use DK weight yarn in your chosen colours.

- Colour 1: Skin (1 ball)
- Colour 2: Stripe A (1 ball)
- Colour 3: Stipe B (1 ball)
- Colour 4: Shirt (1 ball)

MEASUREMENTS

25cm tall

HOOK

3.75mm (US F/5)

DESIGNED BY

AMY KEMBER

Amy is a technical writer living in Ottawa, Canada. Her interest in crochet began when she discovered an amigurumi book in a used bookstore. After making a pig, she was instantly hooked. Since 2010, Amy has been designing and selling her own amigurumi patterns on Etsy.
www.etsy.com/shop/AmysGurumis/

PATTERN
LITTLE BUNNY

HEAD

Using 3.75 mm hook and col 1, make a magic ring.
Rnd 1: 6 dc into ring and pull it closed. (6 sts)
Rnd 2: 2 dc in each dc. (12 sts)
Rnd 3: (1 dc in next dc, 2 dc in the next dc) 6 times. (18 sts)
Rnd 4: (1 dc in each of next 2 dc, 2 dc in next dc) 6 times. (24 sts)
Rnd 5: (1 dc in each of next 3 dc, 2 dc in next dc) 6 times. (30 sts)
Rnd 6: (1 dc in each of next 4 dc, 2 dc in next dc) 6 times. (36 sts)
Rnds 7-13: 1 dc in each dc. (7 rnds of 36 sts)
Rnd 14: (1 dc in each of next 4 dc, dc2tog in next 2 dc) 6 times. (30 sts)
Rnd 15: (1 dc in each of next 3 dc, dc2tog in next 2 dc) 6 times. (24 sts)
Rnd 16: (1 dc in each of next 2 dc, dc2tog in next 2 dc) 6 times. (18 sts)
Rnd 17: (1 dc in next dc, dc2tog in next 2 dc) 6 times. (12 sts)
Fasten off.

BODY

Using col 2, make a magic ring.
Rnd 1: 6 dc into ring and pull it closed. (6 sts)
Rnd 2: 2 dc in each dc. (12 sts)
Rnd 3: (1 dc in next dc, 2 dc in next dc) 6 times. (18 sts)
Change to col 3.
Rnd 4: (1 dc in each of next 2 dc, 2 dc in next dc) 6 times. (24 sts)
Rnd 5: (1 dc in each of next 3 dc, 2 dc in next dc) 6 times. (30 sts)
Change to col 2.
Rnds 6-7: 1 dc in each dc. (2 rnds of 30 sts)
Change to col 3.
Rnds 8-9: 1 dc in each dc. (2 rnds of 30 sts)
Change to col 1.
Rnds 10-11: 1 dc in each dc. (2 rnds of 30 sts)
Rnd 12: (1 dc in each of next 3 dc, dc2tog in next 2 dc) 6 times. (24 sts)
Rnds 13-15: 1 dc in each dc. (3 rnds of 24 sts)
Rnd 16: (1 dc in each of next 2 dc, dc2tog in next 2 dc) 6 times. (18 sts)
Fasten off.

EARS (MAKE 2)

Using col 1, make a magic ring.
Rnd 1: 6 dc into ring and pull it closed.
Rnd 2: 2 dc in each dc. (12 sts)
Rnd 3: (1 dc in next dc, 2 dc in next dc) 6 times. (18 sts)
Rnd 4: (1 dc in each of next 2 dc, 2 dc in next dc) 6 times. (24 sts)
Rnd 5: (1 dc in each of next 3 dc, 2 dc in next dc) 6 times. (30 sts)
Rnd 6: 1 dc in each dc. (30 sts)
Fasten off.

ARMS (MAKE 2)

Using col 1, make a magic ring.
Rnd 1: 4 dc into ring and pull it closed.
Rnd 2: 2 dc in each dc. (8 sts)
Rnds 3-10: 1 dc in each dc. (8 rnds of 8 sts)
Fasten off.

LEGS (MAKE 2)

Using col 2, make a magic ring.
Rnd 1: 5 dc into ring and pull it closed. (5 sts)
Rnd 2: 2 dc in each dc. (10 sts)
Change to col 3.
Rnds 3-4: 1 dc in each dc. (2 rnds of 10 sts)
Change to col 2.
Rnds 5-6: 1 dc in each dc. (2 rnds of 10 sts)
Change to col 3.
Rnds 7-8: 1 dc in each dc. (2 rnds of 10 sts)
Change to col 2.
Rnds 9-10: 1 dc in each dc. (2 rnds of 10 sts)
Change to col 3.
Rnds 11-12: 1 dc in each dc. (2 rnds of 10 sts)
Fasten off.

SHIRT

Using col 4, ch 25, join in 1st ch with ss.
Rnd 1: (1 dc in each of next 4 dc, 2 dc in next dc) 5 times. (30 sts)
Rnd 2: (1 dc in each of next 5 dc, 2 dc in next dc) 5 times. (35 sts)
Rnd 3: (1 dc in each of next 6 dc, 2 dc in next dc) 5 times. (40 sts)
Rnd 4 (make sleeves): skip 11 dc, join in 12th dc with ss, 2 dc in each of next 8 dc, skip 11 dc, join in 32nd dc with ss, 2 dc in each of next 8 dc. (32 sts – do not count the slip sts from this rnd as sts in the following rnd)
Rnds 5-9: 1 dc in each dc. (5 rnds of 32 sts)
Fasten off.

ASSEMBLE THE FACE

Insert 9mm safety eyes between rnd 12 and rnd 13 of the head, and position them 6 sts apart.
Stuff the head firmly.
Cut out a pink felt nose and a cream felt mouth using shapes of your choice.
Glue the nose to the mouth using a hot glue gun. If you don't have a hot glue gun, you can embroider the face on with a yarn of your choice.
Position the mouth and nose between the eyes but slightly higher up on the face between rnd 8 and rnd 12.
Glue the mouth and nose to the face with a hot glue gun.

FINISHING

Stuff the body, arms and legs. Sew the body to the head.
NOTE: There is one extra decrease rnd on the head than on the body so the last rnd of the body should be sewn around the second last rnd on the head.
Sew the arms to the body between rnd 13 and rnd 15, and position them 6 sts apart in the front.
Sew the legs to the body between rnd 4 and rnd 5 and position them 2 sts apart in the front.
Sew the ears to the head between rnd 2 and rnd 4.

Trio of dinosaurs

Step back to the Jurassic era with these adorable dinosaurs

DESIGNED BY

MEVLINN GUSICK

Mevlinn is a college graduate with a BFA in Fine Arts Painting. Her interest in knitting and crochet began when her aunt suggested she try knitting. It peaked her curiosity and here she is today, crocheting amigurumi whenever she gets the chance, and giving them to those she loves.

www.mevvsan.com

DIFFICULTY

✂ ✂ ✂ ✂ ✂

WHAT YOU NEED

- Fibrefill
- 9mm black safety eyes
- Scissors
- Yarn needle
- Stitch marker (optional)
- In this pattern we havae used Rosario 4 Catitano. You will need an aran weight yarn in the following colours:

Colour 1: Green (1 ball)
Colour 2: Dark Green (oddments)
Colour 3: Grey (oddments)

HOOK

2.75mm (US C/2)

MEASUREMENTS

20cm head to tail

PATTERN
STEGOSAURUS

BODY

Using col 1, make a magic ring.
Rnd 1: 7 dc in magic ring. (7 sts)
Rnd 2: 2 dc in each st around. (14 sts)
Rnd 3: (2 dc in next st, 1 dc next st) 7 times. (21 sts)
Rnd 4: (2 dc in next st, 1 dc in next 2 sts) 7 times. (28 sts)
Rnd 5: (2 dc in next st, 1 dc in next 3 sts) 7 times. (35 sts)
Rnd 6: 1 dc in each st around. (35 sts)
Rnd 7: (2 dc in next st, 1 dc in next 4 sts) 7 times. (42 sts)
Rnd 8: 1 dc in each st around. (42 sts)
Rnd 9: 2 dc in next st, 1 dc in next st, 2 dc in next st, 1 dc in next 39 sts. (44 sts)

Note: Rnd 9 is the start of a side specific increase made to create the 'hump' of the Stegosaurus's back. Keep this in mind later when placing the eyes.

Rnd 10: 1 dc in each st around. (44 sts)
Rnd 11: 2 dc in next st, 1 dc in next st, 2 dc in next st, 1 dc in next 41 sts. (46 sts)
Rnds 12-13: 1 dc in each st around. (2 rnds of 46 sts)
Rnd 14: dc2tog, 1 dc in next st, dc2tog, 1 dc in next 41 sts. (44 sts)
Rnd 15: 1 dc in each st around. (44 sts)
Rnd 16: dc2tog, 1 dc in next st, dc2tog, 1 dc in next 39 sts. (42 sts)
Rnd 17: 1 dc in each st around. (42 sts)
Rnd 18: (dc2tog, 1 dc in next 5 sts) 6 times. (36 sts)
Rnd 19: 1 dc in each st around. (36 sts)
Start stuffing and continue stuffing as you go.
Rnd 20: (dc2tog, 1 dc in next 4 sts) 6 times. (30 sts)
Rnd 21: 1 dc in each st around. (30 sts)
Rnd 22: (dc2tog, 1 dc in next 3 sts) 6 times. (24 sts)
Rnd 23: 1 dc in each st around. (24 sts)
Rnd 24: (dc2tog, 1 dc in next 2 sts) 6 times. (18 sts)
Rnds 25-27: 1 dc in each st around. (3 rnds of 18 sts)
Fix safety eyes between rnds 25-27 with 8 sts between each eye.
Rnd 28: (dc2tog, 1 dc in next 7 sts) twice. (16 sts)
Rnd 29: (dc2tog, 1 dc in next 2 sts) 4 times. (12 sts)
Rnd 30: (dc2tog) 6 times. (6 sts)
Fasten off, leaving a tail for sewing. Using wool needle, weave the yarn tail through the front ring of each remaining st and pull it tight to close.

TAIL

Using col 1, make a magic ring.
Rnd 1: 4 dc in magic ring. (4 sts)
Rnd 2: 1 dc in each st around. (4 sts)
Rnd 3: 2 dc in next st, 1 dc in each remaining st to end. (5 sts)
Rnds 4-22: As rnd 3. (24 sts after rnd 22)

Fasten off, leaving a tail for sewing. Stuff the tail and sew it onto the body.

NOTE: When you sew the tail to the body, do so by placing the body on a table and pinning the tail in place first. You want the tail to be attached to the body but touching the table in a completely horizontal position. If you try and sew the tail at an angle to the body you might find that the tail stops the legs from resting on the ground when you later sew them on.

FRONT LEGS (MAKE 2)

Using col 1, make a magic ring.
Rnd 1: 6 dc in magic ring. (6 sts)
Rnd 2: 2 dc in each st around. (12 sts)
Rnd 3 (blo): 1 dcblo in each st around. (12 sts)
Rnds 4-8: 1 dc in each st around. (5 rnds of 12 sts)
Fasten off, leaving a long tail for sewing.

BACK LEGS (MAKE 2)

Using col 1, make a magic ring.
Rnds 1-8: As given for Front Legs. (12 sts)
Rnds 9-10: 1 dc in each st around. (2 rnds of 12 sts)
Fasten off, leaving a long tail for sewing.

SEWING ON THE LEGS

First stuff each leg firmly at the bottom, and less firmly at the top so that you can pinch the opening shut, folding it in half. Now find a spot on the side of the dinosaur where you want to attach the leg. Hold the body while you're doing this and position it above a table. You want the legs to give the body enough lift off the table so that the stomach won't touch the table.

Thread your yarn and sew only the top half of the leg in place. Then sew one row down and continue sewing the rest of the leg in place. It should be very thin at the joint and may be awkward. Instead of fastening off, thread the yarn to the underside of the leg and begin sewing the leg to the body, one st at a time. Go down the leg about 3-5 sts until you see the bowed leg finally tighten up and line up straight with the side of the body. When you are happy with the leg fasten off, and weave the yarn end into the body.

Note: The stegosaurus has longer hind legs than front, so allow for this when attaching them. Always keep in mind how you want your dinosaur's finished position to be when attaching their legs.

SMALL SPIKE (MAKE 6)

Using col 2, make a magic ring.
Rnd 1: 5 dc in magic ring. (5 sts)
Rnd 2: 2 dc in each st around. (10 sts)
Rnd 3: (dc2tog) 5 times. (5 sts)
Fasten off, leaving a long tail for sewing.
Do not stuff the spikes.

MEDIUM SPIKE (MAKE 4)

Using col 2, make a magic ring.
Rnd 1: 5 dc in magic ring. (5 sts)
Rnd 2: 2 dc in each st around. (10 sts)
Rnd 3: (2 dc in next st, 1 dc in next 4 sts) twice. (12 sts)
Rnd 4: (dc2tog, 1 dc in next 4 sts) twice. (10 sts)
Rnd 5: (dc2tog) 5 times. (5 sts)
Fasten off, leaving a long tail for sewing.
Do not stuff the spikes.

LARGE SPIKE (MAKE 2)

Using col 2, make a magic ring.
Rnd 1: 5 dc in magic ring. (5 sts)
Rnd 2: 2 dc in each st around. (10 sts)
Rnd 3: (2 dc in next st, 1 dc in next st) 5 times. (15 sts)
Rnd 4: 1 dc in each st around. (15 sts)
Rnd 5: (dc2tog, 1 dc in next st) 5 times. (10 sts)
Rnd 6: (dc2tog) 5 times. (5 sts)
Fasten off, leaving a long tail for sewing.
Do not stuff the spikes.

FINISHING

Sew the spikes evenly spaced down the body and tail of the Stegosaurus. Starting at the head, you will have two rows of spikes side by side in the following order, working from front to back: Small/Medium/Large/Medium/Small/Small.

The two rows maintain a little over a finger's width apart but narrow more as they reach the tail and head.

TOENAILS

Using col 3, cut a length of yarn about as long as your arm and attach it to the edge of the foot, ch 3, 1 dc back into the same st (one toenail made). *Pull the yarn through as if you were fastening off, but instead thread a needle and move the yarn two sts to the left for the next toenail, ch 3, 1 dc back into the same st; rep from * once more to make the third and final toenail.
Fasten off, weave in all yarn ends.

TAIL SPIKES (MAKE 4)

Using col 3, make a magic ring.
Rnd 1: 4 dc in magic ring. (4 sts)
Rnd 2: 2 dc in next st, 1 dc in each remaining st. (5 sts)
Rnd 3: 1 dc in each st around. (5 sts)
Rnd 4: 2 dc in next st, 1 dc in each remaining st. (6 sts)
Rnd 5: 1 dc in each st around. (6 sts)
Fasten off, leaving a long tail for sewing. Do not stuff the spikes. Sew the spikes to the tip of the dinosaur's tail, two on each side.

DIFFICULTY

✂ ✂ ✂ ✂ ✂

WHAT YOU NEED

- Fibrefill
- 12mm black safety eyes
- Scissors
- Yarn needle
- Stitch marker (optional)
- In this pattern we have used Rosario 4 Catitano. You will need an aran weight yarn in the following colours:

Colour 1: Orange (1 ball)

Colour 2: Light yellow (oddments)

HOOK

2.75mm (US C/2)

MEASUREMENTS

25cm head to tail

PATTERN
T-REX

BODY
Using col 1, make a magic ring.
Rnd 1: 6 dc in magic ring. (6 sts)
Rnd 2: 2 dc in each st around. (12 sts)
Rnd 3: (2 dc in next st, 1 dc in next st) 6 times. (18 sts)
Rnd 4: (2 dc in next st, 1 dc in next 2 sts) 6 times. (24 sts)
Rnd 5: (2 dc in next st, 1 dc in next 3 sts) 6 times. (30 sts)
Rnd 6: (2 dc in next st, 1 dc in next 4 sts) 6 times. (36 sts)
Rnd 7: 1 dc in each st around. (36 sts)
Rnd 8: (2 dc in next st, 1 dc in next 5 sts) 6 times. (42 sts)
Rnds 9-10: 1 dc in each st around. (2 rnds of 42 sts)
Rnd 11: dc2tog, 1 dc in each remaining st to end. (41 sts)
Rnds 12-14: As rnd 11. (38 sts after rnd 14)
Stuff with toy filling and continue stuffing as you go.
Rnd 15: dc2tog, 1 dc in next 33 sts, dc2tog, 1 dc in last st. (36 sts)
Rnd 16: dc2tog, 1 dc in next 31 sts, dc2tog, 1 dc in last st. (34 sts)
Rnd 17: dc2tog, 1 dc in next 29 sts, dc2tog, 1 dc in last st. (32 sts)
Rnd 18: dc2tog, 1 dc in next 27 sts, dc2tog, 1 dc in last st. (30 sts)
Rnd 19: dc2tog, 1 dc in next 25 sts, dc2tog, 1 dc in last st. (28 sts)
Rnd 20: dc2tog, 1 dc in next 23 sts, dc2tog, 1 dc in last st. (26 sts)
Rnd 21: dc2tog, 1 dc in each remaining st to end. (25 sts)
Rnds 22-26: As rnd 21. (20 sts after rnd 26)
Fasten off, leaving a long tail for sewing.

HEAD
Using col 1, make a magic ring.
Rnd 1: 6 dc in magic ring. (6 sts)
Rnd 2: 2 dc in each st around. (12 sts)
Rnd 3: (2 dc in next st, 1 dc in next st) 6 times. (18 sts)
Rnd 4: (2 dc in next st, 1 dc in next 2 sts) 6 times. (24 sts)
Rnd 5: (2 dc in next st, 1 dc in next 3 sts) 6 times. (30 sts)
Rnd 6: (2 dc in next st, 1 dc in next 4 sts) 6 times. (36 sts)
Rnds 7-15: 1 dc in each st around. (9 rnds of 36 sts)
Rnd 16: (dc2tog, 1 dc in next 4 sts) 6 times. (30 sts)
Rnd 17: (dc2tog, 1 dc in next 3 sts) 6 times. (24 sts)
Fix the safety eyes 11 rows down from the magic ring with 13 sts between each eye.
Start stuffing and continue stuffing as you go.
Rnd 18: (dc2tog, 1 dc in next 2 sts) 6 times. (18 sts)
Rnd 19: (dc2tog, 1 dc in next st) 6 times. (12 sts)
Rnd 20: (dc2tog) 6 times. (6 sts)

Fasten off, leaving a tail for sewing. Using yarn needle, weave the yarn tail through the front ring of each remaining st and pull it tight to close. Using the tail end of yarn from the body, sew the head to the body. (The back of the neck should be sewn onto the head approx 6 rnds away from the head's magic ring.)

TAIL
Using col 1, make a magic ring.
Rnd 1: 4 dc in magic ring. (4 sts)
Rnd 2: 1 dc in each st around. (4 sts)
Rnd 3: 2 dc in next st, 1 dc in each remaining st. (5 sts)
Rnds 4-25: As rnd 2. (27 sts after rnd 25)

Fasten off, leaving a long tail for sewing. Stuff the tail with fibrefill and sew it to the body as follows: Place the body on a table in an upright position and pin the tail in place first. If you try to sew the tail on at an angle to the body, you might find that it stops the legs from resting on the ground when you sew them on later.

LEGS (MAKE 2)
Using col 1, make a magic ring.
Rnd 1: 6 dc in magic ring (6 sts)
Rnd 2: 2 dc in each st around. (12 sts)
Rnd 3 (blo): 1 dc in each st around. (12 sts)
Rnds 4-9: 1 dc in each st around. (6 rnds of 12 sts)
Fasten off, leaving a long tail for sewing.

ARMS (MAKE 2)
Using col 1, make a magic ring.
Rnd 1: 4 dc in magic ring. (4 sts)
Rnds 2-7: 1 dc in each st around. (6 rnds of 4 sts)
Fasten off, leaving a long tail for sewing.

FINGERS (MAKE 2)
Using col 1, make a magic ring.
Rnd 1: 4 dc in magic ring. (4 sts)
Rnds 2-3: 1 dc in each st around. (2 rnds of 4 sts)
Fasten off, leaving a long tail for sewing. When both the arms and fingers are complete, sew the finger to the arm so that the end of the arm and the finger are both of equal length. Sew the arms to the body approx 7-8 rows below the point where the head attaches to the body.

TOENAILS
Using col 2, cut a length of yarn about as long as your arm and attach it to the edge of the foot, ch 3, 1 dc back into the same st (one toenail made). *Pull the yarn through two sts to the left for the next toenail, ch 3, 1 dc back into the same st; rep from * once more to make the final toenail.
Fasten off, weave in all yarn ends.

NAIL TIPS
Using col 2, cut a short piece of yarn and pull the yarn through a st at the tip of a finger, ch 1, move the hook to a st to the left of the finger, 1 dc, ch 1, pull the yarn through and fasten off. Weave in the yarn ends gently to avoid distorting the ch 1 tip to the nail you just made.

FINISHING
First stuff each leg firmly at the bottom, and less firmly at the top so that you can pinch the opening shut, folding it in half. Now find a spot on the side of the dinosaur where you want to attach the leg. Hold the body above a table as far as you want it to stand when all the legs are sewn on. Go down the leg about 3-5 sts until you see the bowed leg finally tighten and line up straight with the side of the body. Fasten off and weave in the yarn end.

Note: To keep all legs even you need to attach each leg at the exact same row on the body.

DIFFICULTY

WHAT YOU NEED
- Toy filling
- 12mm black safety eyes
- Scissors
- Wool/tapestry needle
- Stitch marker (optional)

In this pattern we have used Rosario 4 Catitano. You will need an aran weight yarn in the following colours:

Colour 1: Beige (1 ball)
Colour 2 : Brown (oddments)
Colour 3: White (oddments)

HOOK
2.75mm (US C/2)

MEASUREMENTS
25cm head to tail

PATTERN
TRICERATOPS

BODY

Using col 1, make a magic ring.
Rnd 1: 7 dc in magic ring. (7 sts)
Rnd 2: 2 dc in each st around. (14 sts)
Rnd 3: (2 dc in next st, 1 dc next st) 7 times. (21 sts)
Rnd 4: (2 dc in next st, 1 dc in next 2 sts) 7 times. (28 sts)
Rnd 5: (2 dc in next st, 1 dc in next 3 sts) 7 times. (35 sts)
Rnd 6: 1 dc in each st around. (35 sts)
Rnd 7: (2 dc in next st, 1 dc in next 4 sts) 7 times. (42 sts)
Rnds 8-13: 1 dc in each st around. (6 rnds of 42 sts)
Rnd 14: (dc2tog, 1 dc in next 5 sts) 6 times. (36 sts)
Rnd 15: 1 dc in each st around. (36 sts)
Fill with toy filling and continue stuffing as you go.
Rnd 16: (dc2tog, 1 dc in next 7 sts) 4 times. (32 sts)
Rnd 17: 1 dc in each st around. (32 sts)
Rnd 18: (dc2tog, 1 dc in next 6 sts) 4 times. (28 sts)
Rnds 19-20: 1 dc in each st around. (2 rnds of 28 sts)
Fasten off, leaving a tail for sewing.

HEAD

Using col 1, make a magic ring.
Rnd 1: 6 dc in magic ring. (6 sts)
Rnd 2: 2 dc in each st around. (12 sts)
Rnd 3: 1 dc in each st around. (12 sts)
Rnd 4: (2 dc in next st, 1 dc in next st) 6 times. (18 sts)
Rnd 5: 1 dc in each st around. (18 sts)
Rnd 6: (2 dc in next st, 1 dc in next 2 sts) 6 times. (24 sts)
Rnd 7: (2 dc in next st, 1 dc in next 3 sts) 6 times. (30 sts)
Rnd 8: (2 dc in next st, 1 dc in next 4 sts) 6 times. (36 sts)
Rnds 9-11: 1 dc in each st around. (3 rnds of 36 sts)
Rnd 12: 1 dcblo in next 18 sts (this will help you to identify where to crochet the head crest later), 1 dc in each remaining st (working through both rings). (36 sts)
Rnd 13: (dc2tog, 1 dc in next 4 sts) 6 times. (30 sts)
Fix the safety eyes 7 rows down from magic ring with 14 sts between each eye.
Start stuffing and continue stuffing as you go.
Rnd 14: (dc2tog, 1 dc in next 3 sts) 6 times. (24 sts)
Rnd 15: (dc2tog, 1 dc in next 2 sts) 6 times (18 sts)
Rnd 16: (dc2tog, 1 dc in next st) 6 times. (12 sts)
Rnd 17: (dc2tog) 6 times. (6 sts)
Fasten off, leaving a tail for sewing.
Weave the yarn tail through the front ring of each remaining st and pull it tight to close.

HEAD CREST

Using col 1, with the front of the triceratops's head facing you, attach yarn with a sl st to the far right unworked ring from rnd 12 of the head.
Row 1: ch 3 (counts as 1 tr), tr in the same ring at base of ch 3, 1 tr in next 7 rings, 2 tr in next 2 rings, 1 tr in next 7 rings, 2 tr in last ring, turn. (22 sts)
Row 2: ch 2, (counts as 1 htr), 1 htr in same st at base of ch 2, 1 tr in next 9 sts, 2 tr in next 2 sts, 1 tr in next 9 sts, 2 htr in last st, turn. (26 sts)
Row 3: ch 2, 1 htr in same st at base of ch 2, 1 tr in next 11 sts, 2 tr in next 2 sts, 1 tr in next 11 sts, 2 htr in last st, turn. (30 sts)
Change to col 2.
Row 4: *1 dc in next 2 sts, (1 htr, ch 2, 1 htr) in next st; rep from * to end.
Fasten off, weave in ends.

HEAD HORNS (MAKE 2)

Using col 3, make a magic ring.
Rnd 1: 4 dc in magic ring. (4 sts)
Rnd 2: 1 dc in each st around. (4 sts)
Rnd 3: 2 dc in next st, 1 dc in next 3 sts. (5 sts)
Rnd 4: 2 dc in next st, 1 dc in next 4 sts. (6 sts)
Rnd 5: 2 dc in next st, 1 dc in next 5 sts. (7 sts)
Rnd 6: 2 dc in next st, 1 dc in next 6 sts. (8 sts)
Fasten off, leaving a tail for sewing. Lightly fill with toy filling if needed and sew each horn above each eye.

NOSE HORN

Using col 3, make a magic ring.
Rnd 1: 4 dc in magic ring. (4 sts)
Rnd 2: 1 dc in each st around. (4 sts)
Rnd 3: 2 dc in next st, 1 dc in next 3 sts. (5 sts)
Rnd 4: 2 dc in next st, 1 dc in next 4 sts. (6 sts)
Rnd 5: 2 dc in next st, 1 dc in next 5 sts. (7 sts)
Fasten off, leaving a tail for sewing. Lightly stuff with toy filling if needed and sew this horn to the tip of the nose.

Using the tail end of yarn from the body, sew the head to the body.

TAIL

Using col 1, make a magic ring.
Rnd 1: 4 dc in magic ring. (4 sts)
Rnd 2: 1 dc in each st around. (4 sts)
Rnd 3: 2 dc in next st, 1 dc in each remaining st to end. (5 sts)
Rnds 4-21: As rnd 3. (23 sts after rnd 21)
Fasten off, leaving a long tail for sewing. Stuff the tail with toy filling and sew it onto the body as follows:
Place the body onto a table and pin the tail in place first. You want the tail to be attached to the body and be completely horizontal with the

table. If you try to sew the tail on at an angle to the body you might find that the tail stops the legs from resting on the ground when you later sew them on.

FRONT LEGS (MAKE 2)

Using col 1, make a magic ring.
Rnd 1: 6 dc in magic ring. (6 sts)
Rnd 2: 2 dc in each st around. (12 sts)
Rnd 3 (blo): 1 dcblo in each st around. (12 sts)
Rnds 4-9: 1 dc in each st around. (6 rnds of 12 sts)
Fasten off, leaving a long tail for sewing.

BACK LEGS (MAKE 2)

Using col 1, make a magic ring.
Rnds 1-9: As given for Front Legs. (12 sts)
Rnd 10: 1 dc in each st around. (12 sts)
Fasten off, leaving a long tail for sewing.

SEWING ON THE LEGS

Hold the body while you're doing this and position it above a table as far as you want it to stand when all the legs are sewn on. You want the legs to give the body enough lift off the table so that the stomach won't touch the table when it is completely assembled.

First stuff each leg firmly at the bottom, and less firmly at the top so that you can pinch the opening shut, folding it in half. Now find a spot on the side of the dinosaur where you want to attach the leg.

Thread your yarn and sew only the top half of the leg in place. Then sew one row down and continue sewing the rest of the leg in place into this row. It should be very thin at the joint and may be awkward. Instead of fastening off, thread the yarn to the underside of the leg and begin sewing the leg to the body, one st at a time. Go down the leg about 3-5 sts until you see the bowed leg finally tighten and line up straight with the side of the body. When you are happy with the leg, fasten off and weave the yarn end into the body.

NOTE: The triceratops has longer hind legs, and this helps to push its face closer to the ground, so make sure you attach the legs to different rows to make it even. Always keep in mind how you want your dinosaur's finished position to be when attaching their legs.

TOENAILS

Using col 2, cut a length of yarn about as long as your arm, and attach it to the edge of the foot, ch 4, 1 tr back into the same st (one toenail made). *Pull the yarn through as if you were fastening off, but instead thread a needle and move the yarn two sts to the left for the next toenail, ch 4, 1 tr back into the same st; rep from * once more to make the third and final toenail. Fasten off, weave in all yarn ends.

DESIGNED BY

MICHELLE ROBINSON

Michelle is a passionate yarn fondler. She loves to crochet, especially using the Tunisian and tapestry techniques, and she also does a bit of knitting on the side.
www.poppyandbliss.com

Gelato rainbow basket

Add some colour to any room with this beautiful storage basket

DIFFICULTY

✂ ✂ ✂ ✂ ✂

WHAT YOU NEED

- 5mm hook (US H/8)
- Stitch marker
- Yarn needle
- Scissors
- Stitch markers
- Yarn needle
- For this project you will need to use aran weight yarn in your chosen colours. Here we have used Drops Paris in:

Colour 1: Strong Yellow (14) (3 balls)
Colour 2: Medium Pink (33) (1 ball)
Colour 3: Shocking Pink (06) (1 ball)
Colour 4: Light Mint Green (21) (1 ball)
Colour 5: Opal Green (11) (1 ball)
Colour 6: Light Purple (05) (1 ball)
Colour 7: Medium Purple (31) (1 ball)
Colour 8: Light Turquoise (02) (1 ball)
Colour 9: Dark Turquoise (10) (1 ball)
Colour 10: Orange (13) (1 ball)

Note that two strands have been held together throughout this project

MEASUREMENTS

20cm (8in) in diameter and 26cm (10¼in) in height

SPECIAL STITCHES

Blo: Only insert your hook underneath the back loop (the one furthest away from you).

Standing dc: This stitch replaces the usual start of a new round where you would start with a slip stitch and then make 1 chain. Instead, start with a slip knot on hook, insert hook into stitch indicated, yrh and pull up a loop (2 loops on hook), yrh and pull through both loops on hook.

Crab st: This stitch is worked the same as a regular double crochet but is worked in the opposite direction than you would usually work. Ch1 for the start of the round, then *insert hook in next stitch to the right of your hook (or to the left if you are working left-handed), yrh and pull loop through (2 loops on hook), yrh and pull through both loops to complete the crab stitch. Continue around, repeating from * to end. Note that when you insert your hook into each stitch you will need to twist your hand in the same direction as you are working, and point your hook downwards.

PM: Place marker

YRH: Yarn around hook

PATTERN NOTES

- It is up to you how many rows you work after the thumb hole depending on your hands or the hands you are making for. The smaller size here (with 26 sts for hand) fits a small to average women's hand size with average to long finger length.

- To start, make a magic ring as follows: wind yarn around the index finger of your left hand to form a ring, insert hook into ring, yarn around hook and pull a loop through, 1 ch, (does not count as a st), work rnd 1 into the ring, then pull end of yarn tightly to close the hole. Make sure that when you crochet into the ring, that you crochet over the twisted strands of yarn that sit to the left of your hook. Alternatively, you could make 2 ch then work Round 1 into the second chain from hook.

- To keep your circle nice and round, the increases are staggered on alternate rows.

- Work through both loops of stitches unless otherwise indicated.

PATTERN

BASE

Using 2 strands of col 1, make a magic ring, or start with ch2.

Rnd 1 (RS): 6 dc in magic ring (or in 2nd ch from hook). (6 sts)

Rnd 2: 2 dc into each st. (12 sts)

Rnd 3: (1 dc in next st, 2 dc in next st) to end. (18 sts)

Rnd 4: 1 dc in next st, (2 dc in next st, 1 dc in next 2 sts) 5 times, 2 dc in next st, 1 dc in last st. (24 sts)

Rnd 5: (1 dc in next 3 sts, 2 dc in next st) to end. (30 sts)

Rnd 6: 1 dc in next 2 sts, (2 dc in next st, 1 dc in next 4 sts) 5 times, 2 dc in next st, 1 dc in last 2 sts. (36 sts)

Rnd 7: (1 dc in next 5 sts, 2 dc in next st) to end. (42 sts)

Rnd 8: 1 dc in next 3 sts, (2 dc in next st, 1 dc in next 6 sts) 5 times, 2 dc in next st, 1 dc in last 3 sts. (48 sts)

Rnd 9: (1 dc in next 7 sts, 2 dc in next st) to end. (54 sts)

Rnd 10: 1 dc in next 4 sts, (2 dc in next st, 1 dc in next 8 sts) 5 times, 2 dc in next st, 1 dc in last 4 sts. (60 sts)

Rnd 11: (1 dc in next 9 sts, 2 dc in next st) to end. (66 sts)

Rnd 12: 1 dc in next 5 sts, (2 dc in next st, 1 dc in next 10 sts) 5 times, 2 dc in next st, 1 dc in last 5 sts. (72 sts)

Rnd 13: (1 dc in next 11 sts, 2 dc in next st) to end. (78 sts)

Rnd 14: 1 dc in next 6 sts, (2 dc in next st, 1 dc in next 12 sts) 5 times, 2 dc in next st, 1 dc in last 6 sts. (84 sts)

Rnd 15: (1 dc in next 13 sts, 2 dc in next st) to end. (90 sts)

Join with a sl st in next st and fasten off.

SIDES

Note: The first round of each colour is worked into the back loop only (blo) and the second round of the same colour is worked into both loops as usual.

Rnd 1: join col 2 with a standing dc in first st. Working into blo, 1 dc in blo of next 89 sts, do not join. (90 sts)

Rnd 2: PM in first st (this is the standing dc from previous rnd), 1 dc in next 90 sts. Join with a sl st in next st and fasten off. (90 sts)

Rnds 3-36: rep rnds 1-2, changing colour after completing 2 rnds, using the colour numbers in order as listed in yarn list, continuing with col 3 and stopping at col 9 on the second time around. Continue with col 9 to the end. (90 sts)

Rnd 37: PM in first st, 1 dc in next 15 sts, ch15, skip next 15 sts, 1 dc in next 30 sts, ch15, skip next 15 sts, 1 dc in next 15 sts. (60 sts and 2 loops of 15 ch)

Rnd 38: PM in first st, 1 dc in next 15 sts, 1 dc in each of next 15 ch, 1 dc in next 30 sts, 1 dc in each of next 15 ch, 1 dc in next 15 sts. (90 sts)

Rnd 39: 1 dc in each of 90 sts. Join with a sl st in next st, fasten off. (90 sts)

Rnd 40: using only one strand, rejoin yarn in either the same colour or a contrast colour if you prefer. Crab st in each st around, sl st in first crab st to join. (90 sts)

Weave in ends on WS.

TOP TIP

You can crochet over any loose ends in the following round to make them more secure.

DESIGNED BY

ANDREA HARDING

Andrea is the owner and designer of Periwinkle Crochet. She has been designing and teaching crochet since she began crocheting in 2008. She lives with her husband and six children near Sydney, Australia.
@periwinklecrochet
www.ravelry.com/designers/periwinkle-crochet

Ripples wall hanging

Create this stylish, modern wall hanging with a ripple design that will suit any room in your home

DIFFICULTY

✂ ✂ ✂ ✂ ✂

WHAT YOU NEED

- 2mm hook (US B/1)
- Yarn needle
- Scissors
- Stitch markers (1 pink and 1 blue)
- 26x2cm (diameter) dowel for hanging
- Double knitting (8 ply) cotton yarn in your chosen colours. Here have used Bendigo Woollen Mills Cotton 8 ply (100% cotton; 200g/485m), 1 ball in each of:

Colour 1: Peach (20g)
Colour 2: Grey (12g)
Colour 3: Teal (6g)
Colour 4: Parchment (74g)

MEASUREMENTS

21cm (8in) wide; 48cm (19in) high (including fringe, excluding hanger)

TENSION

Not critical for this pattern

SPECIAL STITCHES:

Double crochet back loop only (dcblo) and double crochet 2 together back loop only (dc2togblo): rather than inserting your hook through both loops of the top of the stitch as normal, insert your hook into the back loop only and complete your dc/dc2tog.

All dc2tog and dc2togblo stitches have been modified for this pattern, and are worked over 3 sts as follows:
• dc2tog and dc2togblo – Insert hook into the stitch, yarn over, pull a loop through, sk next stitch, insert hook into the next stitch, yarn over, pull a loop through, yarn over, pull through all 3 stitches on the hook.

PATTERN

Using col 1, ch 67.

Row 1 (RS): Ch 1 (does not count as st throughout), 2 dc in 2nd ch from hook, (1 dc in next 9 sts, dc2tog, 1 dc in next 9 sts*, 3 dc in next st) twice, then rep once more to *, 2 dc in last ch, turn.

Row 2: Ch 1, 2 dc in 1st dc, (1 dc in next 9 sts, dc2tog, 1 dc in next 9 sts*, 3 dc in next st) twice, then rep once more to *, 2 dc in last st, turn.

Row 3: Ch 1, 2 dcblo in 1st dc, (dcblo in next 9 sts, dc2togblo, dcblo in next 9 sts*, 3 dcblo in next st) twice, then rep once more to *, 2 dcblo in last st, turn.

Row 4: Ch 1, 2 dc in 1st dc, (1 dc in next 9 sts, dc2tog, 1 dc in next 9 sts*, 3 dc in next st) twice, then rep once more to *, 2 dc in last st, turn.

Rows 5-10: Rep rows 3 and 4 three times and work last yoh of row 10 in col 2.

Rows 11-16: Rep rows 3 and 4 three times and work last yoh of row 16 in col 3.

Rows 17-26: Rep rows 3 and 4 five times and work last yoh of row 26 in col 4.

Rows 27-30: Rep rows 3 and 4 twice and work last yoh of row 30 in col 1.

Rows 31-38: Rep rows 3 and 4 four times and work last yoh of row 38 in col 3.

Rows 39-44: Rep rows 3 and 4 three times and work last yoh of row 44 in col 2.

Rows 45-46: Rep row 3 and 4 and mark last st of row 46 with a pink stitch marker.

Row 47: Ch 1, sk 1st st, 1 dcblo in next 9 sts, dc2togblo, 1 dcblo in next 9 sts, mark the next st with a blue stitch marker, turn and continue on these sts only.

Row 48: Sk 1st st, 1 dc in next 7 sts, dc2tog, 1 dc in next 7 sts, turn.

Row 49: Sk 1st st, 1 dcblo in next 5 sts, dc2togblo, 1 dcblo in next 5 sts, turn.

Row 50: Sk 1st st, 1 dc in next 3 sts, dc2tog, 1 dc in next 3 sts, turn.

Row 51: Sk 1st st, 1 dcblo in next st, dc2togblo, 1 dcblo in next st. Fasten off.

** Using col 2, attach yarn to the back loop of the blue marked stitch. Rep rows 47-51 **

Rep from ** to ** once more, but don't mark the stitch.

Using col 2, attach yarn to the last stitch of row 46 (pink marked stitch), ch 1, 1 dc into the end of each row along the top edge. Fasten off and weave in the ends.

PATTERN NOTES

- Chains at the start of a round do not count as stitches.
- Keep stitches fairly firm to create a dense fabric with no gaps.
- To change colours, work the last yarn over of the previous stitch in the new colour.
- You can alter the depth of the stripes by changing the number of rows in each colour; changing colour at the end of an even-numbered row is best.
- Odd-numbered rows are the right side of the crochet; even numbered rows are the wrong side of the crochet.

BLOCKING

Blocking will give a neat, flat, even look to your project, while making it easier to keep the correct shape.
Place the crochet onto the ironing board wrong side up. Cover with a clean cloth and gently steam. Leave flat until dry and cool.

FRINGE

Each fringe piece uses 2 strands of col 4.

Cut 134 strands at 33cm (13in) each. Fold 2 strands of yarn in half, forming a loop at one end. Take your hook and draw the loop through the st that you're attaching the fringe to. Draw the loose ends of the yarn through the loop. Gently pull the fringe to tighten.

Once all tassels are attached, iron fringe straight then trim into a V shape.

HANGING

Sew the crochet onto the dowel, looping the yarn through every 3rd st along the top edge. Weave in ends.

Attach a piece of yarn to either end of the dowel for hanging.

Clothes

102
Summer diamonds toddler dress

106
Rainbow scarf

108
Snappy slippers

112
Cosy cobbles earwarmer

114
Horizon jumper

120
Crossed stitch fingerless gloves

124
Find-your-rhythm beanie

128
Pyjama-eating elephant

Summer diamonds toddler dress

With its playful design and easy wearability, the summer diamonds toddler dress is ready for an afternoon of fun

DIFFICULTY

✂ ✂ ✂ ✂ ✂

WHAT YOU NEED

- 4.5mm hook (US 7)
- Yarn needle
- Scissors
- Stitch markers
- For this project you will need to use DK yarn. Here we have used We Are Knitters Cotton Wool in Khaki. The yardage will depend on which size dress you are making.

MEASUREMENTS

(In inches)

24mo:
Body Circumference 28.25
Neckline 5.75
Body Length 16.25
Length to Armhole 14.5

2T:
Body Circumference 30
Neckline 6.25
Body Length 16.25
Length to Armhole 14.25

3T:
Body Circumference 32
Neckline 6.5
Body Length 16.25
Length to Armhole 14

TENSION

14 sts and 9 rows to measure 10x10cm (4x4in) over double crochet using 4.5mm hook.

SPECIAL STITCHES:

Foundation double crochet – First stitch: Ch 2, insert hook into first ch, yoh and and pull up a loop, yoh, pull through one loop on hook (1 chain stitch made), yoh, pull through 2 loops on hook. All other stitches: insert hook into ch-1 st made by previous st, yoh and pull up a loop, yoh, pull through one loop on hook (1 ch st made), yoh, pull through 2 loops on hook.

Foundation treble crochet – First stitch: Ch 3, yoh, insert hook into first ch, yoh and pull up a loop, yoh, pull through one loop on hook (1 chain stitch made), [yoh, pull through 2 loops on hook] twice. All other stitches: Yoh, insert hook into ch-1 st made by previous st, yoh and pull up a loop, yoh, pull through one loop on hook (1 ch st made), [yoh, pull through 2 loops on hook] twice.

PATTERN

BODY

FIRST HALF

For all sizes, work 57 foundation treble crochet stitches. Turn.

Row 1: Ch 2, 1 tr in each of next 6 sts, (ch 1, sk 1 st, 1 tr in next st, ch 1, sk 1 st, 1 tr in each of next 11 sts) 3 times, ch 1, sk 1 st, 1 tr in next st, ch 1, sk 1 st, 1 tr in each of next 6 sts. Turn. (57 sts)

Row 2: Ch 2, 1 tr in each of next 5 sts, (ch 1, sk 1 st, 1 tr in each of next 3 sts, ch 1, sk 1 st, 1 tr in each of next 9 sts) 3 times, ch 1, sk 1 st, work 1 tr in each of next 3 sts, ch 1, sk 1 st, work 1 tr in each of next 5 sts. Turn. (57 sts)

Row 3: Ch 2, 1 tr in each of next 4 sts, (ch1, sk 1 st, 1 tr in each of next 5 sts, ch 1, sk 1 st, 1 tr in each of next 7 sts) 3 times, ch 1, sk 1 st, 1 tr in each of next 5 sts, ch1, sk 1 st, 1 tr in each of next 4 sts. Turn. (57 sts)

Row 4: Ch 2, 1 tr in each of next 3 sts, (ch1, sk 1 st, 1 tr in each of next 7 sts, ch 1, sk 1 st, 1 tr in each of next 5 sts) 3 times, ch 1, sk 1 st, 1 tr in each of next 7 sts, ch1, sk 1 st, 1 tr in each of next 3 sts. Turn. (57 sts)

Row 5: Ch 2, 1 tr in each of next 2 sts, (ch1, sk 1 st, 1 tr in each of next 9 sts, ch1, sk 1 st, 1 tr in each of next 3 sts) 3 times, ch 1, sk 1 st, 1 tr in each of next 9 sts, ch 1, sk 1 st, 1 tr in each of next 2 sts. Turn. (57 sts)

Row 6: Ch 2, 1 tr in next st, (ch1, sk 1 st, 1 tr in each of next 11 sts, ch1, sk 1 st, 1 tr in next st) 3 times, ch 1, sk 1 st, 1 tr in each of next 11 sts, ch1, sk 1 st, 1 tr in next st. Turn. (57 sts)

Row 7: Ch 2, 1 tr in each of next 2 sts, (ch1, sk 1 st, 1 tr in each of next 9 sts, ch1, sk 1 st, 1 tr in each of next 3 sts) 3 times, ch 1, sk 1 st, 1 tr in each of next 9 sts, ch1, sk 1 st, 1 tr in each of next 2 sts. Turn. (57 sts)

Row 8: Ch 2, 1 tr in each of next 3 sts, (ch1, sk 1 st, 1 tr in each of next 7 sts, ch1, sk 1 st, 1 tr in each of next 5 sts) 3 times, ch 1, sk 1 st, 1 tr in each of next 7 sts, ch1, sk 1 st, 1 tr in each of next 3 sts. Turn. (57 sts)

Row 9: Ch 2, 1 tr in each of next 4 sts, (ch1, sk 1 st, 1 tr in each of next 5 sts, ch1, sk 1 st, 1 tr in each of next 7 sts) 3 times, ch 1, sk 1 st, 1 tr in each of next 5 sts, ch1, sk 1 st, 1 tr in each of next 4 sts. Turn. (57 sts)

Row 10: Ch 2, 1 tr in each of next 5 sts, (ch1, sk 1 st, 1 tr in each of next

DESIGNED BY

CHIWEI RANCK

ChiWei Ranck is the creative engine behind One Dog Woof, a fiber arts company where the timeless craft of knit and crochet meet the demands of modern living. One Dog Woof creates designs that are purposeful, sophisticated and fun.
www.1dogwoof.com
@1dogwoof

PATTERN NOTES

- The whole idea of the construction is to create the front and back of the dress as one solid piece sideways, leaving slits for the armholes. The body piece is then sewn to the neck piece, again leaving space for the armholes.
- The length of the dress, which uses the diamond motif, is always worked in multiples of 14 + 1.
- On the neck piece, work the foundation double crochet stitch in the round. When joining to the first stitch, turn your work counter clockwise, and place the active yarn above your row. Make sure there are no twists in your work, and join to the first dc with a ss. Afterwards, you'll need to sew the beginning tail to the round and close up the joining seam.
- When working dc stitches along the side of the diamond motif, we worked 2 dc into the side of each tr stitch.
- Use a mattress stitch to sew the body to the neck piece.

3 sts, ch1, sk 1 st, 1 tr in each of next 9 sts) 3 times, ch 1, sk 1 st, 1 tr in each of next 3 sts, ch1, sk 1 st, 1 tr in each of next 5 sts. Turn. (57 sts)
Rows 11-20: Repeat Rows 1-10.

24 mo Sizes only:
Rows 21-29: Repeat Rows 1-9.

2T, 3T Sizes only:
Rows 21-30: Repeat Rows 1-10.
Rows 31-31 (33): Repeat Rows 1-1 (3).

Split for Armhole, All Sizes:
Row 1: Work 1 tr in each st across. (57 sts)
Row 2: Work 1 slip st in each of next 51 (50, 49) sts, ch 8 (9, 10). Turn.
Row 3: Starting with 3rd chain from hook, work 1 tr in each st across (this is 1 tr in each of 6 (7, 8) chain sts then 1 tr in each of 51 (50, 49) body sts). Turn. (57 sts)

SECOND HALF

Rows 1-29 (31, 33): Beginning with Row 3 (5, 7), continue in pattern as established from First Half.
Row 30 (32, 34): 1 tr in each st across. Turn. (57 sts)

To seam the dress, bring the beginning edge up to align with Row 30 (32, 34). Starting from the bottom, mattress stitch up 51 (50, 49) sts to leave second arm opening. Fasten off and weave in ends.

Join yarn with a standing dc into the top of body piece (where the arm splits are), then work 62 (66, 70) dc evenly across the top (1 st per row). Fasten off and weave in ends. Repeat for the other side of the body piece.

NECK PIECE

Work 64 (72, 80) foundation double crochet sts. Join to first double crochet st.
Row 1: Ch 1, starting in same st, work 1 dc in each st around. Join to first dc with ss. (64 (72, 80) sts)
Row 2: Ch 2 (does not count as st), starting in same st, work 1 tr in each st around. Join to first tr with ss. (64 (72, 80) sts)
Row 3: Ch 1, starting in same st, work 1 dc in each st around. Join to first dc with ss. (64 (72, 80) sts)
Row 4: Ch 1, starting in same st, work 1 dc in each of next 11(13, 16) sts (armhole), (1 dc, ch 2) 20 (22, 23) times (neckline), 1 dc in each of next 12 (14, 17) sts (armhole), (1 dc, ch 2) 20 (22, 23) times (neckline), 1 dc in next st. Join to first dc with a ss. Fasten off and weave ends. (64 (72, 80) sts)

ASSEMBLY

Align the neckline portion of the neck piece with the body and sew together with a whip stitch or a mattress stitch. You'll want to work the stitches evenly across and close together so you don't leave gaps in the connection. You can work into the dc of the body piece and into the chain spaces of the neck piece. Fasten off and weave in ends. Turn the dress around and repeat for the other side.
Note: If you're unsure about the assembly, do the back side first to work out any issues, then work the front neckline cleanly.

BOTTOM SCALLOP BORDER

Row 1: Work a standing dc into the bottom of the dress by one of the seams, then work 124 (132, 140) dc evenly around the bottom of the dress. Join to first dc with ss.
Row 2: *Ch 6, sk 4 dc, 1 dc into next st, rep from * around. Join with ss into base of first ch-6.
Row 3: Work 1 ss into next 3 chains, *ch 6, 1 slip stitch into next ch-6 space, rep from * around. Join with ss into base of first ch-6. Fasten off and weave in ends.

Rainbow scarf

The perfect accessory to inject a little bit of colour into the darker days of winter

DIFFICULTY

WHAT YOU NEED

- 4.5mm hook (US 7)
- Yarn needle
- Fibrefill stuffing
- A pair of 10mm black safety eyes
- You will need to use DK yarn in your chosen colour. Here we have used Deramores Studio DK in:

Colour 1: Wisteria
Colour 2: Sherbet
Colour 3: Spring Green
Colour 4: Lemon
Colour 5: Apricot

MEASUREMENTS

CHILD SIZE:
Length: approx. 120cm (47in)
Width (when flat): 10cm (4in)
ADULT SIZE:
Length: approx. 165cm (65in)
Width (when flat): 12.5cm (5in)

TENSION

21.5 stitches and 16.5 rounds measure 10x10cm (4x4in) in dc (blo), using 4mm hook and DK weight yarn

COLOUR BLOCK NOTES:

CHILD: The child size requires 200 rounds to achieve the desired length; changing colour every 20 rounds will give you 10 colour blocks i.e. 2 blocks of each of your 5 colours

ADULT: The adult size requires 270 rounds to achieve the desired length; changing colour every 18 rounds will give you 15 colour blocks i.e. 3 blocks of each of your 5 colours

Feel free to adjust the stripe sequence any way you like!

PATTERN

Using col 1, make a slip knot and leave a long tail. Ch 44 [54]. Being careful not to twist the chain, join to the first ch with a ss to form a loop.

Rnd 1 (RS): Ch 1 (does not count as a st throughout), 1 dc (blo) in same ch as ss just made (place a stitch marker in this dc), 1 dc (blo) in each ch around until you reach the stitch marker. Do not join to this 1st dc with a ss. (44 [54] sts)

Continue to work in a spiral without joining.

Rnd 2: 1 dc (blo) in marked stitch (now move the stitch marker up to dc just made), 1 dc (blo) in each st until the end of the round (when you reach the stitch marker). Do not join to the 1st dc. (44 [54] sts)

FOR CHILD SIZE

Rnds 3-20: Rep rnd 2, change to col 2 on last st of rnd 20. (44 sts)

Rnds 21-40: Using col 2, rep rnd 2, change to col 3 on last st of rnd 40. (44 sts)

Rnds 41-60: Using col 3, rep rnd 2, change to col 4 on last st of rnd 60. (44 sts)

Rnds 61-80: Using col 4, rep rnd 2, change to col 5 on last st of rnd 80. (44 sts)

Rnds 81-100: Using col 5, rep rnd 2, change to col 1 on last st of rnd 100. (44 sts)

Rnds 101-200: Following colour sequence as set, rep rnd 2, changing colours every 20 rnds. (44 sts)

Fasten off and leave a long tail.

ADULT SIZE

Rnds 3-18: Rep rnd 2, change to col 2 on last st of rnd 18. (54 sts)

Rnds 19-36: Using col 2, rep rnd 2, change to col 3 on last st of rnd 36. (54 sts)

Rnds 37-54: Using col 3, rep rnd 2, change to col 4 on last st of rnd 54. (54 sts)

Rnds 55-72: Using col 4, rep rnd 2, change to col 5 on last st of rnd 72. (54 sts)

Rnds 73-90: Using col 5, rep rnd 2, change to col 1 on last st of rnd 90. (54 sts)

Rnds 91-270: Following colour sequence as set, rep rnd 2, changing colours every 18 rnds. (54 sts)

Fasten off and leave a long tail.

FINISHING

At both ends of the scarf, weave the tail in and out between the stitches of the first and last rounds. Pull tail to close up the hole and add a couple of whipstitches to secure each end.

Sew a pom pom at each end.

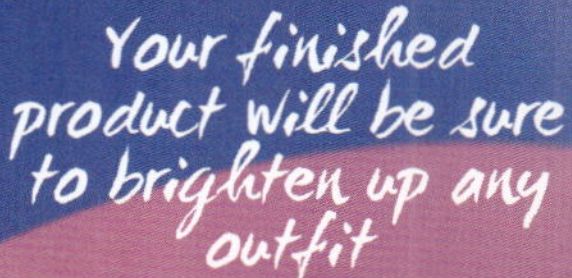

DESIGNED BY

SARAH RUANE

Sarah is a crochet designer and all-round lover of making stuff. She likes to be very intentional with what she creates and designs - everything must be going to a good home or fulfilling a purpose in her own home! *nedandmimi.com*

PATTERN NOTES

- The scarf is crocheted in the round to create a long tube.
- Instructions are given for the child size, with the adult size given in brackets: [ ]
- At the end of each round, do not join to the previous round; continue working in a spiral.
- When changing colours, switch to the new colour on the last yarn over at the end of the round. Cut the yarn for the previous colour.

TOP TIP

To make the scarf wider, adjust your starting chain by any number. Every 4 extra stitches will add approximately 2cm to the overall finished width.

Snappy slippers

Cosy and warm and perfect for the whole family, these slippers will hug your feet!

DIFFICULTY

✂ ✂ ✂ ✂ ✂

WHAT YOU NEED

- 6mm hook (US J)
- Yarn needle
- Chunky (bulky) yarn in one colour, 110-183m (120-200yds) based on size

MEASUREMENTS

To fit approximate foot lengths 20 (23, 25, 28, 30)cm (8 (9, 10, 11, 12) in); pattern is written for smallest size with changes for other sizing in parentheses.

TENSION

10 htr and 8.5 rows to measure approximately
10 x 10cm (4 x 4in) using chunky yarn and 6mm hook

SPECIAL STITCHES:

FPtr: Front Post treble crochet: yoh, insert hook around the post to be worked, from front to back to front again, and work a treble crochet.

PATTERN

FOR MEDIUM WIDTH approx 25cm (10in) around foot (make 2)

TOE/FOOT SECTION

Round 1: Ch 4, join with ss to first ch to form a ring, ch 1, work 10 dc into centre of the ring, join. (10 sts)
Round 2: Ch 1, 2 htr in each st, join. (20 sts)
Round 3: Ch 1, (1 htr in next 3 sts, 2 htr in next st) 5 times, join. (25 sts)
Round 4: Ch 1, 1 htr in each st, join. (25 sts)
Repeat Round 4 until piece measures 11.5 (14, 16.5, 17.75, 20.25) cm (4.5 (5.5, 6.5, 7, 8)in).

HEEL SECTION FOR 20CM (8IN) SLIPPER

Row 1 (Right Side Row): Ch 1, 1 htr in next 15 sts, turn. (15 sts)
Row 2: Ch 1, 1 htr in each st, turn. (15 sts)
Row 3: Ch 1, 1 htr in next st, 2 htr in next st, 1 htr in each st until there are 2 sts left, 2 htr in next st, 1 htr in last st, turn. (17 sts)
Row 4: Repeat row 2. (17 sts)
Row 5: Repeat row 3. (19 sts)
Row 6: Ch 1, 1 htr in next 8 sts, 1 dc in next st, sk next st, 1 dc in next st, 1 htr in next 8 sts (Figure 1). (18 sts)
Put right sides of slippers together, matching sts at heel, working through sts in both ends. Ss centre back heel seam together (Figure 2). Fasten off.
SKIP TO ANKLE BAND

FOR 23CM (9IN) SLIPPER

Following pattern for heel section of 20cm (8in) slipper, work to the end of row 4. (17 sts)
Rows 5-6: Repeat rows 3 & 4. (19 sts)
Next, work row 6 and sew heel as given for 20cm (8in) slipper.
SKIP TO ANKLE BAND

FOR 25CM (10IN) SLIPPER

Following pattern for heel section of 20cm (8in) slipper, work to the end of row 3. (17 sts)
Rows 4-5: Repeat row 2. (17 sts)
Row 6: Repeat row 3. (19 sts)
Row 7: Repeat row 2. (19 sts)
Next, work row 6 and sew heel as given for 20cm (8in) slipper.
SKIP TO ANKLE BAND

DESIGNED BY

MARIA BITTNER

Maria loves to design fun and functional crochet pieces that can be customised and fit today's modern aesthetic.
www.pattern-paradise.com
@patternparadise

FOR 28 CM (11IN) SLIPPER

Row 1 (Right Side Row): Ch 1, 1 htr in next 15 sts. (15 sts)
Row 2: Ch 1, turn, 1 htr in each st. (15 sts)
Row 3: Repeat row 2. (15 sts)
Row 4: Ch 1, turn, 1 htr in next st, 2 htr in next st, 1 htr in each st until there are 2 sts left, 2 htr in next st, 1 htr in next st. (17 sts)
Rows 5-6: Repeat row 2. (17 sts)
Row 7: Repeat row 4. (19 sts)
Row 8: Repeat row 2. (19 sts)
Next, work row 6 and sew heel as given for 20cm (8in) slipper.
SKIP TO ANKLE BAND

FOR 30CM (12IN) SLIPPER

Following pattern for heel section of 28cm (11in) slipper, work to the end of row 6. (17 sts)
Rows 7-9: Repeat rows 4-6. (19 sts)
Next, work row 6 and sew heel as given for 20cm (8in) slipper.

ANKLE BAND

(Figure 3)
Rnd 1: Join yarn at back seam, ch 1, 1 dc in side of each row and each st all around top of slipper, join. (22 (24, 26, 28, 30) sts)
Rnd 2: Ch 1, 1 htr in each st, join. (22 (24, 26, 28, 30) sts)
Rnd 3: Ch 1, (1 FPtr in next st, 1 htr in next st) to end, join. (22 (24, 26, 28, 30) sts)
Rnd 4: Repeat row 3.
Rnd 5: Ch 1, (1 FPtr in next st, 1 dc in next st) to end, join. 22 (24, 26, 28, 30) sts)
Fasten off.

FOR NARROW WIDTH approx 20cm (8in) around foot

(make 2)

Fig: 1

TOP TIP

This piece would also look great in a variegated yarn and, depending upon the size of the ball, can usually be completed from one ball of yarn

match up stitches and slip stitch back seam closed

TOE/FOOT SECTION

Rnd 1: Ch 4, join with ss to first ch, ch 1, work 10 dc into the r ng, join. (10 sts)
Rnd 2: Ch 1, 2 htr in each st, join. (20 sts)
Rnd 3: Ch 1, 1 htr in each st, join. (20 sts)
Repeat rnd 3 until piece measures 11.5 (14, 16.5, 17.75, 20.25)cm (4.5 (5.5, 6.5, 7, 8)in).

HEEL SECTION FOR 20CM (8IN) SLIPPER

Row 1 (Right Side Row): Ch 1, 1 htr in next 11 sts, turn. (11 sts)
Row 2: Ch 1, 1 htr in each st, turn. (11 sts)
Row 3: Ch 1, 1 htr in next st, 2 htr in next st, 1 htr in each st until there are 2 sts left, 2 htr in next st, 1 htr in next st, turn. (13 sts)
Row 4: Repeat row 2. (13 sts)
Row 5: Repeat row 3. (15 sts)
Row 6: Ch 1, 1 htr in next 6 sts, 1 dc in next st, sk next st, 1 dc n next st, 1 htr in last 6 sts (Figure 1). (14 sts)
Put right sides of slippers together, matching sts at heel, working through sts in both ends, ss centre back heel seam together (Figure 2). Fasten off.
SKIP TO ANKLE BAND

FOR 23CM (9IN) SLIPPER

Following pattern for heel section of 20cm (8in) slipper, work to the end of row 4. (13 sts)
Rows 5-6: Repeat rows 3-4. (15 sts)
Next, work row 6 and sew heel as given for 20cm (8in) slipper (narrow width).
SKIP TO ANKLE BAND

FOR 25CM (10IN) SLIPPER

Following pattern for heel section of 20cm (8in) slipper, work to the end of row 3. (13 sts)
Rows 4-5: Repeat row 2. (13 sts)
Row 6: Repeat row 3. (15 sts)
Row 7: Repeat row 2. (15 sts)
Next, work row 6 and sew heel as given for 20cm (8in) slipper (narrow width).
SKIP TO ANKLE BAND

FOR 28CM (11IN) SLIPPER

Row 1 (Right Side Row): Ch 1, 1 htr in next 11 sts. (11 sts)
Row 2: Ch 1, turn, 1 htr in each st. (11 sts)
Row 3: Repeat row 2. (11 sts)
Row 4: Ch 1, turn, 1 htr in next st, 2 htr in next st, 1 htr in each st until there are 2 sts left, 2 htr in next st, 1 htr in next st. (13 sts)
Rows 5-6: Repeat row 2. (13 sts)
Row 7: Repeat row 4. (15 sts)
Row 8: Repeat row 2. (15 sts)
Next, work row 6 and sew heel as given for 20cm (8in) slipper (narrow width).
SKIP TO ANKLE BAND

FOR 30CM (12IN) SLIPPER

Following pattern for heel section of 28cm (11in) slipper, work to the end of row 6. (13 sts)
Rows 7-9: Repeat rows 4-6. (15 sts)
Next, work row 6 and sew heel as given for 20cm (8in) slipper (narrow width).

ANKLE BAND

(Figure 3)
Rnd 1: Join yarn at back seam, ch 1, 2 dc in side of first row, 1 dc in side of each remaining row and each st all around top of slipper, join. (22 (24, 26, 28, 30) sts)
Work as given for Ankle band of Medium Width Slipper from rnd 2 to end.

FOR WIDE WIDTH approximately 28cm (11in) around foot (make 2)

TOE/FOOT SECTION

Rnd 1: Ch 4, join with ss to first ch, ch 1, work 10 dc into the ring, join. (10 sts)
Rnd 2: Ch 1, 2 htr in each st, join. (20 sts)
Rnd 3: Ch 1, (1 htr in next 4 sts, 2 htr in next st) 4 times, join. (24 sts)
Rnd 4: Ch 1, (1 htr in 5 sts, 2 htr in next st) 4 times, join. (28 sts)
Rnd 5: Ch 1, 1 htr in each st, join. (28 sts)
Repeat rnd 5 until piece measures 11.5 (14, 16.5, 17.75, 20.25)cm (4.5 (5.5, 6.5, 7, 8)in).

Fig:3

HEEL SECTION
FOR 20CM (8IN) SLIPPER

Row 1 (Right Side Row): Ch 1, 1 htr in next 17 sts, turn. (17 sts)
Row 2: Ch 1, 1 htr in each st, turn. (17 sts)
Row 3: Ch 1, 1 htr in next st, 2 htr in next st, 1 htr in each st until there are 2 sts left, 2 htr in next st, 1 htr in next st, turn. (19 sts)
Row 4: Repeat row 2. (19 sts)
Row 5: Repeat row 3. (21 sts)
Row 6: Ch 1, 1 htr in first 9 sts, 1 dc in next st, sk next st, 1 dc in next st, 1 htr in next 9 sts (Figure 1). (20 sts)
Put right sides of slippers together, matching sts at heel, working through sts in both ends, ss centre back heel seam together (Figure 2). Fasten off.
SKIP TO ANKLE BAND

FOR 23CM (9IN) SLIPPER

Following pattern for heel section of 20cm (8in) slipper, work to the end of row 4. (19 sts)
Rows 5-6: Repeat rows 3-4. (21 sts)
Next, work row 6 and sew heel as given for 20cm (8in) slipper (wide width).
SKIP TO ANKLE BAND

FOR 25CM (10IN) SLIPPER

Following pattern for heel section of 20cm (8in) slipper, work to the end of row 3. (19 sts)
Rows 4-5: Repeat row 2. (19 sts)
Row 6: Repeat row 3. (21 sts)
Row 7: Repeat row 2. (21 sts)
Next, work row 6 and sew heel as given for 20cm (8in) slipper (wide width).
SKIP TO ANKLE BAND

FOR 28CM (11IN) SLIPPER

Row 1 (Right Side Row): Ch 1, 1 htr in next 17 sts, turn. (17 sts)
Row 2: Ch 1, 1 htr in each st, turn. (17 sts)
Row 3: Repeat row 2. (17 sts)
Row 4: Ch 1, 1 htr in next st, 2 htr in next st, 1 htr in each st until there are 2 sts left, 2 htr in next st, 1 htr in next st, turn. (19 sts)
Rows 5-6: Repeat row 2. (19 sts)
Row 7: Repeat row 4. (21 sts)
Row 8: Repeat row 2. (21 sts)
Next, work row 6 and sew heel as given for 20cm (8in) slipper (wide width).
SKIP TO ANKLE BAND

FOR 30CM (12IN) SLIPPER

Following pattern for heel section of 28cm (11in) slipper, work to the end of row 6. (19 sts)
Rows 7-9: Repeat rows 4-6. (21 sts)
Next, work row 6 and sew heel as given for 20cm (8in) slipper (wide width).

ANKLE BAND

(Figure 3)
Rnd 1: Join yarn at back seam, ch 1, 2 dc in side of first row, 1 dc in side of each remaining row and each st all around top of slipper, join. (24 (26, 28, 30, 32) sts)
Work as given for Ankle band of Medium Width Slipper from rnd 2 to end.

PATTERN NOTES

- The pattern is written in 5 sizes and 3 widths.

- The beginning ch 1 does not count as a stitch.

- The toe/foot section and ankle band are worked in the round.

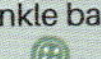

- Join rounds with a slip stitch to the first stitch of the round.
- Weave ends as you work.

Cosy cobbles earwarmer

Keep your ears warm while staying on trend whatever your style

DESIGNED BY
SHELLEY WORTH
Shelley loves crocheting items that are practical as well as pretty and that can be enjoyed by others.
etsy.com/uk/shop/HumblyCraftedShop
@humbly.crafted

DIFFICULTY

✂ ✂ ✂ ✂ ✂

WHAT YOU NEED

- 10mm hook (US N/15)
- Yarn needle
- Scissors
- Tape measure
- Super chunky (super bulky) yarn in your chosen colours. Here we have used approximately 70g of Stylecraft Special Chunky in Silver and Pale Rose. (Other weights of yarn can be substituted but this may affect the starting chain.)

MEASUREMENTS

Chain length 49.5cm (19.5in) to fit average teen-adult.

TENSION

Approximately 13 sts to measure 10cm over pattern, using 4mm hook and super chunky yarn.

SPECIAL STITCHES

Double crochet into the back bump: when working the initial stitches into the chain, work your dc into the back bump of the chain (along the underside of the chain) rather than into the 'V'.

Double crochet back loop only (dcblo): rather than inserting your hook through both loops of the stitch as normal, insert your hook into the back loop only and complete your dc.

PATTERN NOTES

- The ch-1 at the start of each row does not count as a stitch.
- Stitches are worked into both loops as normal, unless stated otherwise.

PATTERN

Leaving a long tail of approximately 25cm (10in), loosely ch 39.
(Always ensure that your starting ch is a multiple of 2 + 1 for the turning chain).

Row 1 (RS): 1 dc into the back loop only of the 2nd ch from hook and in each ch to the end, turn. (Stitch count should match your original chain minus the turning chain e.g. original chain length of 39 - 1 = 38 sts)
Row 2: Ch 1 (does not count as a st throughout), (1 tr in first st, 1 dc in next st) to end, turn. You should end on a dc. (38 sts)
Row 3: Ch 1, 1 dcblo in first st and in each st to end of row, turn. (38 sts)

Rep rows 2 and 3 respectively, twice more or until your earwarmer reaches your desired depth (ensure that you end after row 3). Fasten off, leaving a long tail of approximately 25cm (10in).

JOINING

Bring the two short ends together with the right sides (textured side) facing inwards. Thread your needle with the tail from your starting ch and whip stitch the two ends together. Weave in your end and snip.
Turn your earwarmer inside out so the right side is now facing you.

DESIGN OPTIONS

Option 1: Simply weave in your other tail end of yarn, to leave a flat seam so that your earwarmer is the same thickness all the way around.
Option 2: Gather your earwarmer together along the seam and wrap your other tail end around it to create the cinch. We began wrapping from the back as this creates the neatest cinch, but do what works best for you. To secure the yarn in place, thread the end of the tail through the knot from the bottom to the top twice and then weave the end in on the wrong side.
This option can be worn with the cinched section in the middle of your forehead or off to the side.

Insert your hook into the back bump of the chain

DESIGNED BY

LITTLE GOLDEN NOOK

Sandra has been crocheting and designing patterns for seven years, and has written a number of garment patterns for adults and children featuring the popular bobble stitch.
www.ravelry.com/designers/little-golden-nook
@littlegoldennook

Horizon jumper

Make sure your little ones stay warm and snug

PATTERN NOTES

• There are instructions for five different sizes in this jumper: ages 2, 4, 6, 8 and 10. The stitch counts at the end of the rows will be written as follows: (2, 4, 6, 8, 10 sts).

• 5.5mm hook is used for jumper.

• 4mm hook is only used for neckband.

DIFFICULTY

✂ ✂ ✂ ✂ ✂

WHAT YOU NEED

- 5.5mm (US I/9) hook
- 4mm (US G/6) hook
- Yarn needle
- You will need to use aran (worsted weight) yarn in a main colour. The amount needed varies, depending on the size you are making:
- Age 2: 500m
- Age 4: 600m
- Age 6: 700m
- Age 8: 800m
- Age 10: 950m
- You will also need 10m of 4 contrast colours.

MEASUREMENTS

Finished chest measurements are: 60 (68, 74, 80, 84)cm (23½ (27, 29, 31, 33)in)

Back length: 42 (44, 50, 55, 60)cm (16½, 17, 20, 23½)in)

TENSION

12 rows and 13 sts to measure 10x10cm (4x4in) over htr using a 5.5mm hook

SPECIAL STITCHES:

Bobble stitch (also called tr5tog): Yo and insert hook into stitch or space, yo and pull up a loop, yo and pull through first 2 loops (2 loops left on hook), *yo insert hook into same into the same stitch or space as before, yo and pull up a loop, yo and pull through first two loops only (3 loops left on the hook), repeat from * 3 times more (6 loops now on hook), yo and pull through all those 6 loops. Stitch is complete.

Your next stitch after a bobble st will be the hdc.

For contrast colour bobbles, complete the stitch before the bobble in main colour in full, yo using contrast colour (CC) and, leaving a long tail to secure later, then insert into stitch and work the bobble stitch until you have 6 loops on your hook (1 loop in main colour and 5 loops in contrast colour), drop contrast colour and work a yo in main colour and complete the stitch in main colour.

PATTERN

FRONT RIBBING

Chain 44, (48, 52, 56, 60) depending on the size you're making.

Row 1: 1 htr in 3rd ch from hook, 1 htr in each ch to end, turn. (42, 46, 50, 54, 58 sts)

Rows 2-3: Ch 2 (not counted as a st), (1 FPhtr around next st, 1 BPhtr around next st) to end, turn. (42, 46, 50, 54, 58 sts)

BODY

Row 4: Ch 1 (not counted as a st throughout), 1 dc in each st to end, turn. (42, 46, 50, 54, 58 sts)

Rows 5-24: Ch 1, 1 htr in each st to end, turn. (42, 46, 50, 54, 58 sts)

BOBBLE ROWS

MC - main jumper colour

CC - contrast colour

Prepare your contrast colours for your bobble rows. You can use up to 4 different colours.

Note that if you are using different yarn weights to your MC or have a preference for less bulky bobbles work fewer partial treble crochets (i.e. tr4tog instead of tr5tog).

After each bobble stitch and htr in MC ensure that you pull CC strands to tighten the bobble and avoid loose bobble loops.

Row 1: Ch 1, work 1 bobble in CC in next st, 1 htr in MC in next st, *1 bobble in CC in next st, 1 htr in MC in next st*, repeat from * to * to end, turn. (42, 46, 50, 54, 58 sts)

Row 2: Ch 1, using MC, 1 dc in each st to end, turn. (42, 46, 50, 54, 58 sts)

Row 3: Repeat row 1, using a different colour for bobbles, if desired. (42, 46, 50, 54, 58 sts)

Row 4: Repeat row 2. (42, 46, 50, 54, 58 sts)

SHAPE SLEEVES

Row 5: 1 ss in each of next 4 sts, ch 1, 1 bobble in CC in SAME STITCH, 1 htr in MC in next st, *1 bobble in CC in next st, 1 htr in MC in next st*, repeat from * to * until you have 3 sts remaining, turn. (36, 40 44, 48, 52 sts)

TOP TIP

For smaller sizes try using DK/lightweight yarn and a 4.5mm hook (we suggest making size 2 for 6-12 months, and size 4 for 12-18 months).

Row 6: Repeat row 2. (36, 40 44, 48, 52 sts)
Row 7: last bobble row: Ch 1, *1 bobble in CC in next st, 1 htr in MC in next st*, repeat from * to * to end, turn. (36, 40 44, 48, 52 sts)
Rows 8-17 (17, 19, 19, 21): Ch 1, 1 htr in each st to end, turn. (36, 40, 44, 48, 52 sts)

NECKLINE

Right side of neck
Row 1: Ch 1, 1 htr in next 9 (9, 10, 10, 11) sts, htr2tog, turn. (10, 10, 11, 11, 12 sts)
Row 2: Ch 1, htr2tog, 1 htr in each st to end, turn. (9, 9, 10, 10, 11 sts)
Row 3: Ch 1, 1 htr in next 7 (7, 8, 8, 9) sts, htr2tog, turn. (8, 8, 9, 9, 10 sts)
Row 4: Ch 1, htr2tog, 1 htr in each st to end. (7, 7, 8, 8, 9 sts)

Fasten off, leaving a long tail for sewing shoulders

Left side of neck
Attach yarn to stitch 11 (11, 12, 12, 13) from the left side.
Row 1: Ch 1, starting in the same stitch as the join, 1 htr2tog, 1 htr in each st to end, turn. (10, 10, 11, 11, 12 sts)
Row 2: Ch 1, 1 htr in each st to last 2 sts of left neckline, htr2tog, turn. (9, 9, 10, 10, 11 sts)
Row 3: Ch 1, htr2tog, 1 htr in each st to end, turn. (8, 8, 9, 9, 10 sts)
Row 4: Repeat row 2. (7, 7, 8, 8, 9 sts)

Fasten off, leaving a long tail for sewing shoulders.

BACK

For the back piece you will add the bottom ribbing at the end of the piece later.

Ch 34 (38, 42, 46, 50).
Row 1: 1 htr in 3rd chain from hook, 1 htr in each ch to end, turn. (32, 36, 40, 44, 48 sts)
Row 2: Ch 1, 2 htr in first stitch, 1 htr in each stitch to last st, 2 htr in last stitch, turn. (34, 38, 42, 46, 50 sts)
Rows 3-6: Repeat row 2. (42, 46, 50, 54, 58 sts)
Rows 7-29 (31, 35, 39, 43): Ch 1, 1 htr in each st to end, turn. (42, 46, 50, 54, 58 sts)

SLEEVE INDENT

Next row: 1 ss in each of next 4 sts, ch 1, 1 htr in same st, 1 htr in every st until you have 3 sts remaining, turn. (36, 40, 44, 48, 52 sts)
For the next 19 (20, 20, 20, 22) rows: Ch 1, 1 htr in every st to end, turn. (36, 40, 44, 48, 52 sts)
Final row neck shaping: Ch 1, 1 htr in the next 6 (6, 7, 7, 8) sts, htr2tog, fasten off. Reattach yarn to stitch 8 (8, 9, 9, 10) from the opposite side, ch 1, htr2tog, 1 htr in each stitch to end, fasten off.

BACK RIBBING

To add the ribbing to the bottom of your back piece, attach yarn to the side where the increase finishes (at row 5), ch 1 and 1 dc in next stitch.
Row 1: After this dc, htr evenly around the arch, and in each st along the bottom, and then evenly up the arch of the other side, finishing with 1 dc in the side of row 4 and ss in side of row 5 (from the back instructions), turn. (44, 52, 54, 58, 62 sts)
Row 2: Ch 1, sk current stitch, 1 dc around back post of next stitch (this is the dc), *1 FPhtr around next st, 1 BPhtr around next st*, repeat from * to * until you reach the starting dc from row 1, 1 dc around front/back post depending where you are up in the sequence, ss in next st, turn. (44, 52, 54, 58, 62 sts)
Row 3: Ch 1, ss into dc from previous row, keeping rib pattern correct, alternate between 1 FPhtr and 1 BPhtr across to dc stitch on other side, ss into dc and into next stitch, fasten off. (42, 50, 54, 56, 60 sts)

SLEEVES (MAKE 2)

For your sleeves you will be increasing at both ends, for a few rows to begin with.

Ch 23 (25, 27, 29, 31).
Row 1: 1 htr in 3rd chain from hook, 1 htr in each ch across, turn. (21, 23, 25, 27, 29 sts)

Row 2: Ch 2 (does not count as st), (1 FPhtr around next st, 1 BPhtr around next st) to last st, 1 FPhtr around last st, turn. (21, 23, 25, 27, 29 sts)
Row 3: Ch 2 (does not count as st), (1 BPhtr around next st, 1 FPhtr around next st) to last st, 1 BPhtr around last st, turn. (21, 23, 25, 27, 29 sts)
Row 4: Ch 1, 2 dc in first st, 1 dc in each st to last st, 2 sc in last st, turn. (23, 25, 27, 29, 31 sts)
Row 5: Ch 1, 1 dc in first stitch, *ch 1, sk 1 st, 1 dc in next st*, repeat from * to * to end, (thus ending with dc), turn. (23, 25, 27, 29, 31 sts)
Row 6: increase row: Ch 1, (1 dc, ch 1, 1 dc) in first stitch, *ch 1, skip ch-sp, 1 dc in next st*, repeat from * to * to last ch-sp and dc, ch 1, skip ch-sp, (1dc, ch1, 1dc) in last dc, turn. (27, 29, 31, 33, 35 sts)
NOTE: includes ch-sp in stitch count
You will now be increasing every 4 (4, 4, 5, 5) rows

The following are instructions for size 2 (4, 6) only:
Row 7: Ch 1, 1 dc in first st, ch 1, skip ch-sp, *1 dc in next stitch (into dc from previous row), ch 1, skip ch-sp*, repeat from * to * to last st, 1dc in last st, turn. (27, 29, 31, 33, 35 sts)
Rows 8-10: Repeat row 7.
Row 11: Repeat row 6. (31, 33, 35 sts)
Rows 12-13: Repeat row 7.
Row 15: Repeat row 6. (35, 37, 39 sts)
Rows 16-18: Repeat row 7.
Row 19: Repeat row 6. (39, 41, 43 sts)
From now on you will be increasing every 5 (5, 5) rows
Rows 20-23: Repeat row 7
Row 24: Repeat row 6. (43, 45, 47 sts)

The following are instructions for size (8, 10) only:
Rows 7-10: Repeat row 7.
Row 11: Repeat row 6. (37, 39 sts)
Rows 12-15: Repeat row 7.
Row 16: Repeat row 6. (41, 43 sts)
Rows 17-20: Repeat row 7.
From now on you will increase every 6 rows.
Row 21: Repeat Row 6. (45, 47 sts)
Rows 22-26: Repeat row 7. (49, 51 sts)

BOTH SIZES

Continue in pattern, increasing as per row 6, every 5 (5, 5, 6, 6) rows, keeping an eye on your length and width as indicated in the diagram. Once you reach the required width, continue in the pattern WITHOUT increasing (thus repeating row 7 only) until length is reached.
Approx final stitch count 45 (49, 57, 65, 71) sts, depending on tension/gauge.

MAKING UP

To sew together, use whip stitch with right sides facing. Start by sewing shoulders together, then sew your sleeves to the sides where the indents are. Sew each side (leaving 'V' open at the bottom), and then sew sleeve seams.

NECKBAND

Using 4mm hook, join yarn onto neckline at shoulder seam, ch 1 dc evenly around neck opening, including 6 x dc2tog spread along the sides of the neckline as pictured (2 at either side of the neck front where the neckline slants, 1 at either side of back of neck where the neckline slants), ss to first dc, do not fasten off. (52, 56, 62, 66, 68 sts)

The neckband is now worked sideways around the neck edge, and is joined onto the main neckband with a ss after each alternate row:

Step 1: Ch 6, 1 dc in 2nd ch from hook, 1 dc in next 4 ch (5 sts).
You are now back at neckline. These 5 sts just worked create the depth/height of the neckband.
Step 2: Ss in each of next 2 sts of neckline, ch1, turn your work.
Step 3: Skip the 2 slipped sts just worked, 1 dcblo in each of the 5 sts of neckband, ch 1 turn, 1 dcblo in each of the 5 sts on neckband. Your hook is now at the neckline.
Repeat Steps 2-3 all around the neckline then ss the seam together.
Final approximate row
band count is 54 (58, 64, 68, 72) rows.

Note that your back piece will be longer than your front piece so that the bottom will dip below the ribbing for the front

"Customise the jumper with different colours for all the children in your life"

Crossed stitch fingerless gloves

Keep your hands fashionably warm in the cold weather

DIFFICULTY

✂ ✂ ✂ ✂ ✂

WHAT YOU NEED

- 5.5mm hook (US J/10) for main body of glove
- 4mm hook (US H/8) for rib
- Yarn needle
- You will need to use approximately 80m of aran or chunky weight yarn in your chosen colour. Here we have used Drops Big Merino in:

Colour 1: Orange (1 ball)

MEASUREMENTS

These gloves fit an average woman's hand, but the pattern can be adjusted to fit other sizes.

TENSION

Tension is not critical but if you aim for approximately 13.5 sts per 10cm (4in) over pattern, you will achieve the measurements given.

SPECIAL STITCHES

Crossed half treble crochet: Skip 1 st, 1 htr in next st, 1 htr back into skipped st, working in front of htr just made.

PATTERN NOTES

- It is up to you how many rows you work after the thumb hole depending on your hands or the hands you are making for. The smaller size here (with 26 sts for hand) fits a small to average women's hand size with average to long finger length.
- Stitch counts are also included for a larger size – where patterns say 26/28 sts, this is 26 sts for smaller size and 28 sts for larger size.

PATTERN

WRISTBAND RIB

With smaller hook, ch 10.

Rnd 1 (RS): 1 dc in 2nd ch from hook, 1 dc in next 8 sts, turn. (9 sts)

Rows 2-26: Ch1 (does not count as st), 1 dc in back loop only of next 9 sts, turn. (9 sts)

Note: If you need more width for your wrist, add two more rows.

Fold your cuff in half with wrong sides together, and slip stitch ends together to form the wrist (sl st through front loop only so that your back loops form a rib effect when turned inside out).

Turn your wrist piece right side in ready to crochet your first round of the body section.

MAIN SECTION

Note that if you added one or two rows more of rib, you will have 28 sts in total after rnd 1.

Rnd 1 (RS): Ch 1 (does not count as a st throughout), 1 dc in same place as beg ch 1, work 26/28 dc evenly around by working 1 dc in each rib row-end. (26/28 sts)

Switch to 5.5mm hook.

Note that you will end rnd 2 with 14 crossed sts if you started with 28 sts.

Rnd 2: Ch 1, skip st at base of beg ch 1, 1 htr in next stitch, 1 htr back into the skipped st (and working in front of the last htr), *skip 1 st, 1 htr into next st, 1 htr back into the skipped st; rep from * around, until you have 13/14 crossed sts, sl st in beginning ch 1. (26/28 sts)

Rnds 3-5: Rep rnd 2. (26/28 sts)

CREATE THUMBHOLE: RIGHT-HAND GLOVE

Rnd 6: Work as given for rnd 2 until you have 4 sts remaining, ch 4 loosely, skip the last 4 sts and sl st in beg ch 1. (22/24 sts and a ch4-sp)

Rnd 7: Work as given for rnd 2 until you reach the 4 ch, skip 1st ch, 1 htr in 2nd ch, 1 htr back into the skipped ch, skip 3rd ch, 1 htr in 4th ch, 1 htr back into the skipped 3rd ch,
sl st in beg ch 1 to join. (26/28 sts)

DESIGNED BY

LITTLE GOLDEN NOOK

Sandra has been crocheting and designing patterns for seven years, and she has written a number of garment patterns for adults and children featuring the popular bobble stitch.
@littlegoldennook
www.ravelry.com/designers/little-golden-nook

CREATE THUMBHOLE: LEFT-HAND GLOVE

Rnd 6: Ch 1, skip 1st st, 1 htr in next st, 1 htr back into the skipped st to form 1 crossed htr, ch 4 loosely, skip 5 sts, 1 htr in next st, 1 htr back into the 5th skipped st, *skip next st, 1htr in next st, 1htr back into skipped st; rep from * to end, sl st in beg ch 1 to join. (22/24 sts and a ch4-sp)

Rnd 7: Ch 1, skip 1st st, 1htr in next st, then 1 htr back into skipped st, now work along the 4 ch, skip 1st ch, 1 htr in 2nd ch, 1 htr in the skipped 1st ch, skip 3rd ch, 1htr in 4th ch, 1htr in skipped 3rd ch, *skip 1 st, 1 htr in next st, then 1 htr back into the skipped st; rep from * to end. (26/28 sts).

FOR BOTH GLOVES

Rnds 8-9: Rep rnd 2. (26/28 sts)

Rnd 10 (optional): Rep Rnd 2 but working crossed double crochets instead of htr, to add a fraction more length to your gloves if needed. (26/28 sts)

Fasten off and weave in ends.

TOP TIP

This pattern can be adapted for children by using DK yarn with a 4mm hook for the main section and a 3.5mm hook for the ribbing.

Find-your-rhythm beanie

With just one ball of chunky yarn, you can make a warm and cosy hat that is perfect for a last-minute handmade gift

DIFFICULTY

WHAT YOU NEED

- 6mm hook (US J/10)
- Stitch marker
- Pompom maker (optional as you can also use your hands to make a pompom)
- Yarn needle
- You will need to use chunky weight yarn in your chosen colour. Here we have used West Yorkshire Spinners Re:treat in:

Colour 1: Bliss (0692) (1 ball)

Colour 2: Unwind (094) (1 ball)

MEASUREMENTS

51cm (20in) circumference, but will stretch to fit up to a medium adult head size of 55cm (21¾in). Depth is approximately 22cm (8¾in), but is adjustable and can be made longer by adding more rounds.

TENSION

12.5 sts and 10 rows measure 10 x 10cm (4 x 4in) over htr pattern, using 6mm hook.

SPECIAL STITCHES

Crab stitch: working in the opposite direction than a standard double crochet, insert hook into next stitch to the right of your hook if you are a right-handed crocheter or to the left of your hook if you are a left-handed crochet (you will need to point your hook downwards and into the stitch), yarn around hook and pull a loop through (2 loops on hook), yarn around hook and pull through 2 loops to complete your crab stitch.

PATTERN NOTES

- For rounds 18-20, you will only insert your hook into the back loop of each stitch. This leaves the front loop free, which creates a decorative line.

PATTERN

Using col 1 and 6mm hook, make a magic ring.

Rnd 1 (RS): ch 1 (not counted as a st), 10 htr into the ring. (10 sts)

Continue to work in a spiral without joining each round or turning. Place a stitch marker in the first stitch of each round, moving it up as you work. This will help to mark the end of each round.

Rnd 2: 2 htr in each st to end of round. (20 sts).

Rnd 3: (1 htr in next st, 2 htr in next st) 10 times. (30 sts)

Rnd 4: (1 htr in each of next 2 sts, 2 htr in next st) 10 times. (40 sts)

Rnd 5: (1 htr in each of next 3 sts, 2 htr in next st) 10 times. (50 sts)

Rnd 6: (1 htr in each of next 4 sts, 2 htr in next st) 10 times. (60 sts)

Rnd 7: (1 htr in each of next 14 sts, 2 htr in next st) 4 times. (64 sts)

Rnds 8-17: 1 htr in each st around.

Rnds 18-20: 1 htr in back loop only of each st around.

Note that if you would prefer a more slouchy beanie, you can add extra rounds here, by repeating the last round two or three times more (there is enough yarn for this).

After last round, sl st in next st (going under both loops).

Rnd 21: Border: ch 1 (not counted as a st), 1 crab stitch in each stitch around (see special stitches), sl st in first crab stitch to join.

Note that the crab stitch isn't essential; it simply provides a decorative edge. You could use a standard double crochet edge instead.

Fasten off and weave in ends. Add a pompom either using a medium or large pompom maker, or use your hands as follows:

Wrap chosen yarn around the palm of your hand, approximately 50-60 times. The more you wrap, the thicker your pompom will be (you may need to wrap yarn more times if you use a thinner yarn from your stash). Carefully remove the wraps from your hand and tie a length of matching yarn tightly around the centre.

Snip the folded ends of yarn and shake your pompom before trimming into a rounded shape. Use the tail ends of yarn to sew your pompom to your beanie at the centre top of hat.

DESIGNED BY

LYNNE ROWE

Lynne is a knitting and crochet technical editor and designer based in Cheshire, UK. She enjoys teaching and passing on her skills to others, so that they can improve their wellbeing with knitting and crochet.
@the_woolnest
www.knitcrochetcreate.com

TOP TIP

If you would like the brim of your beanie to feel snug, you could change down to a 5.5mm hook for the last few rounds.

Pyjama-eating elephant

Encourage kids to keep their bedrooms tidy by 'feeding' the pyjama-eating elephant with their pyjamas

DIFFICULTY

✂ ✂ ✂ ✂ ✂

WHAT YOU NEED

- 8mm hook (US L/11)
- 4mm hook (US G/6)
- 5.5mm hook (US I/9)
- 5mm hook (US H/8))
- Yarn needle
- Stitch markers or contrast thread
- Fibrefill stuffing
- You will need to use super chunky yarn in your chosen colours. Here we have used Lion Brand Hometown USA (100% acrylic; 140g/74m) in:
  - Colour 1: Dallas Grey (1 ball)
  - Colour 2: Miami Seafoam (1 ball)
- You will also need small amounts of:
  - Colour 3: Aran yarn in pink or red (55m)
  - Colour 4: Double knitting yarn in black (2.75m)

MEASUREMENTS

23x30cm (9x11¾in)

TENSION

Body: 9 sts and 11 rows to measure 10x10cm (4x4in), over double crochet using 8mm hook and super chunky yarn.

Lining: 12 sts and 7 rows to measure 10x10cm (4x4in), over double crochet using 5.5mm hook and worsted weight yarn.

SPECIAL STITCHES:

dc2tog – insert hook in next st, yoh and pull up a loop, insert hook in the following st, yoh and pull up a loop again, yoh and pull through all 3 loops on your hook.

tr2tog – yoh, insert hook in next st, yoh and pull up a loop, yoh and pull up through 2 loops on the hook, yoh again and insert hook in next st, yoh and pull up a loop, yoh and pull up through 2 loops on the hook, yoh and pull through all 3 loops on your hook.

PATTERN

LINING

This goes inside the pyjama eater and is sewn onto the mouth. If you are a skilled seamstress you can make the lining from fabric instead.

The lining is crocheted in a round, so at the end of each round join to 1st st of the round (top of ch 3) with ss. The starting ch-3 of each round counts as 1 tr, so make your next tr in next available st. If the pattern directs you to make 1st tr at the bottom of ch-3, this is to increase the st count.

Using col 3 and 5.5mm hook, ch 15.

Rnd 1 (RS): 2 tr in 4th ch from hook (skipped 3 ch counts as 1 tr), 1 tr in next 10 sts, 6 tr in last st, rotate your work and continue making the following sts along the bottom loops of the chain: 1 tr in next 10 sts, 3 tr in last st. (32 sts)

Rnd 2: Ch 3, 1 tr in bottom of ch-3 (in the place you joined), 2 tr in next 2 sts, 1 tr in next 10 sts, 2 tr in next 6 sts, 1 tr in next 10 sts, 2 tr in next 3 sts. (44 sts)

Rnd 3: Ch 3, 1 tr in next 43 sts. (44 sts)

Rnd 4: Ch 3, 1 tr in bottom of ch-3 (in the place you joined), 1 tr in next 20 sts, 2 tr in next 2 sts, 1 tr in next 20 sts, 2 tr in next st. (48 sts)

Rnd 5: Ch 3, 1 tr in next 47 sts. (48 sts)

Rnd 6: Ch 3, tr2tog, 1 tr in next 18 sts, tr2tog, 1 tr in next 2 sts, tr2tog, 1 tr in next 18 sts, tr2tog, 1 tr in next st. (44 sts)

Rnd 7: Ch 3, 1 tr in next 43 sts. (44 sts)

Rnd 8: Ch 3, tr2tog, 1 tr in next 16 sts, tr2tog, 1 tr in next 2 sts, tr2tog, 1 tr in next 16 sts, tr2tog, 1 tr in next st. (40 sts)

Rnd 9: Ch 3, 1 tr in next 39 sts. (40 sts)

Rnd 10: Ch 3, tr2tog, 1 tr in next 14 sts, tr2tog, 1 tr in next 2 sts, tr2tog, 1 tr in next
14 sts, tr2tog, 1 tr in next st. (36 sts)

Rnd 11: Ch 3, 1 tr in next 35 sts. (36 sts)

Rnd 12: Ch 3, 1 tr in next 17 sts, 1 dc in next 18 sts. (36 sts)

FINISHING

Fasten off leaving around 76cm (30in) tail for sewing the lining to the mouth, once row 12 of the front part is completed. Weave in the starting tail securely. Lining size is 20cm (8in) wide (in the widest point) x 18cm (7in) high.

EYES (MAKE 2)

Eyes are crocheted in a round.

DESIGNED BY

ANETA WAWRO

Aneta specialises in designing unique and modern items for babies and kids. Her mission is to write her patterns in a way that everyone will be able to follow with ease and achieve the best result possible.
@crochetarcade
www.crochetarcade.co.uk

Using col 4 and 4mm hook, make a magic ring or ch 2 and work into 2nd ch.
Rnd 1 (RS): Work 6 dc into the ring. (6 sts)
Join to 1st st and fasten off leaving about 20cm (8in) tail for sewing on the eyes. Tighten the magic ring and weave in the starting tail end securely. Finished eye's diameter should be around 1.7cm (¾in).

ELEPHANT'S BODY - FRONT PART

The body is made out of 2 pieces (front and back) and joined together with ss. Both parts are made in rows. Turn at the end of each row. Ch 1 at the start of the row is a turning chain and it doesn't count as a stitch, so always make the first stitch of the row in the first available stitch.
Using col 1 and 8mm hook, ch 8.
Row 1 (RS): 2 dc in 2nd ch from hook, 1 dc in next 5 sts, 2 dc in next st. (9 sts)
Row 2: Ch 1, 2 dc in next st, 1 dc in next 7 sts, 2 dc in next st. (11 sts)
Row 3: Ch 1, 2 dc in next st, 1 dc in next 9 sts, 2 dc in next st. (13 sts)
Row 4: Ch 1, 2 dc in next st, 1 dc in next 11 sts, 2 dc in next st. (15 sts)
Row 5: Ch 1, 1 dc in next 15 sts. Turn your work over and mark sts number 6 and 10 with a stitch maker or piece of contrasting colour yarn. This is where you will sew on the eyes later. (15 sts)
Rows 6-7: Ch 1, 1 dc in next 15 sts. (15 sts)
Row 8: Ch 1, dc2tog, 1 dc in next 11 sts, dc2tog. (13 sts)
Row 9: Ch 1, 1 dc in 1st st, ss in next st, ch 9, sk 9 sts on the head and ss in 12th st, 1 dc in last st. (13 sts)
Row 10: Ch 1, 1 dc in 1st st, sk next st, 1 dc in back loops of next 2 sts, ss in back loops of next 5 sts, 1 dc in back loops of next 2 sts, sk next st, 1 dc in last st but when doing last yoh, pull up col 2 to start the next round with. (11 sts)
Row 11: Ch 1, 2 dc in 1st st and when working last yoh of 2nd st pull up col 1, 1 dc in next 9 sts and when doing last yoh of 9th st pull up col 2, 2 dc in next st. (13 sts)

Note: You can crochet over the yarn ends and the working yarn of the colour you are not currently using (but will need to pick up again in the same row). Alternatively, you can just leave the loose yarn from colour changes hanging on the WS, as they won't be visible.
Row 12: Ch 1, 2 dc in 1st st, 1 dc in next 11 sts, 2 dc in next st. (15 sts)

Place the eyes on the centre of marked sts 6 & 10 of round 5. Thread the yarn tail on to blunt ended yarn needle and sew on the eyes using whip stitch, inserting the needle through top of the sts on the eyes and catching the surface of the sts on the head (close to the edge of the eyes). Use remaining yarn to embroider the eyebrows over 2 dc sts (slightly on an angle), one row above the eye.

Take your hook off the loop and enlarge it (so it doesn't unravel) before sewing the lining to the mouth opening (gap between rows 9 & 10). Thread the yarn tail from the lining onto a yarn needle and sew the lining to the WS using whip stitch. There are a total of 18 sts around the mouth and twice as many (36 sts) on the lining, so attach every 2 sts of the lining to each 1 st of the mouth. Proceed sewing all 18 tr sts to the 9 sts of the top lip, then sew on remaining 18 dc sts to the 9 sts of the bottom lip. Note: Insert the needle under both loops on the lining and only under the front loop on the mouth. Fasten off and weave in remaining end in the lining. Insert your hook back in the working loop of the front part and tighten in. Proceed to make the rest of the front. (See Fig 1.)

Rows 13-15: Ch 1, 1 dc in next 15 sts. (15 sts)
Row 16: Ch 1, 2 dc in 1st st, 1 dc in next 13 sts, 2 dc in next st. (17 sts)
Rows 17-18: Ch 1, 1 dc in next 17 sts. (17 sts)
Row 19: Ch 1, 2 dc in 1st st, 1 dc in next 15 sts, 2 dc in next st. (19 sts)
Rows 20-21: Ch 1, 1 dc in next 19 sts. (19 sts)
Row 22: Ch 1, dc2tog, 1 dc in next 15 sts, dc2tog. (17 sts)
Rows 23-24: Ch 1, 1 dc in next 17 sts. (17 sts)
Row 25: Ch 1, dc2tog, 1 dc in next 13 sts, dc2tog. (15 sts)
Row 26: Ch 1, 1 dc in next 15 sts. (15 sts)
Row 27: Ch 1, (dc2tog) twice, 1 dc in next 7 sts, (dc2tog) twice. (11 sts)
Row 28: Ch 1, (dc2tog) twice, 1 dc in next 3 sts, (dc2tog) twice. (7 sts)

Fig 1

FINISHING
CROCHETING A BORDER

Do NOT cut off the yarn but continue making dc sts around the entire front part of the body (with RS facing). Make 1 dc in each side of the row until you get to the head part made in col 1. You should end up with 17 dc. When doing last yoh of the 17th st, pull up col 1 through last 2 loops on hook. Continue working dc around the head; you should have 27 sts in col 1. When doing last yoh of the 27th st, pull up col 2 through last 2 loops on the hook. Continue working dc in col 2 until you get to the point where you started. You will end up with further 17 sts on the side of the rows and 7 sts at the bottom (on top of row 27). To summarise you will have 68 dc around the entire front part of the body (17 in col 2 + 27 in col 1 + 24 in col 2). Fasten off and weave in the ends inside the sts of the same colour on the WS.

ELEPHANT'S BODY - BACK PART

Using col 1, ch 8.
Row 1: 2 dc in 2nd ch from hook, 1 dc in next 5 sts, 2 dc in last st. (9 sts)
Row 2: Ch 1, 2 dc in 1st st, 1 dc in next 7 sts, 2 dc in next st. (11 sts)
Row 3: Ch 1, 2 dc in 1st st, 1 dc in next 9 sts, 2 dc in next st. (13 sts)
Row 4: Ch 1, 2 dc in 1st st, 1 dc in next 11 sts, 2 dc in next st. (15 sts)
Rows 5-7: Ch 1, 1 dc in next 15 sts. (15 sts)
Row 8: Ch 1, dc2tog, 1 dc in next 11 sts, dc2tog. (13 sts)
Row 9: Ch 1, dc in next 13 sts. (13 sts)
Row 10: Ch 1, dc2tog, 1 dc in next 9 sts, dc2tog (when working last yoh of the decrease, pull up col 2). (11 sts)
Row 11: Ch 1, 2 dc in 1st st, 1 dc in next 9 sts, 2 dc in next st. (13 sts)
Row 12: Ch 1, 2 dc in 1st st, 1 dc in next 11 sts, 2 dc in next st. (15 sts)
Rows 13-28: Repeat rows 13-28 of front part. (7 sts)

FINISHING

Do not fasten off but crochet a border in the same way as on the front part. Do NOT cut the yarn after you finish the border, so you can continue joining front and back together in the next step. Before you start joining the 2 parts together, weave in all the yarn ends from chaining the colours on the WS (WS of the back should be the same as the WS of the front part).

JOINING FRONT PART TO BACK

Continue where you left off and start joining the back part to the front part of the body by working ss through both parts at the same time, sewing them at the same time. Make sure the WS of each part is facing each other. You could choose to insert your hook underneath both loops on each part (total 4 loops on top of the hook) or just through 2 closest loops (back loop of back part and front loop of front part). The second option will result in a flatter seam. Alternatively, you can sew parts with needle and whip stitch, which will give the flattest seam.

When you get to the head part made in col 1, switch the colour by pulling col 1 when making a previous ss. Then switch back to col 2 when you get to the end of the head in the same way. About 10 sts before you completely close the body, stuff the head of the pyjama eater with fibrefill. Join the remaining sts and on the end, ss to the first st and fasten off. Weave in all the ends.

EARS

Start by leaving around 30cm (12in) tail before the slip knot for sewing the ears to the body. Ears are worked in rows.

RIGHT EAR:
Using col 1 and 8mm hook, ch 7.
Row 1 (RS): 1 dc in 2nd ch from hook, 1 dc in next 4 sts, 2 dc in next st. (7 sts)
Row 2: Ch 2 (does not count as st), 1 htr in next 3 sts, 1 dc in next 4 sts. (7 sts)
Row 3: Ch 1, 2 dc in 1st st, 1 dc in next 3 sts, 1 htr in next 2 sts, 1 tr in next st. (8 sts)
Row 4: Ch 2 (does not count as st), 1 htr in next 3 sts, 1 dc in next 4 sts, 2 dc in next st. (9 sts)
Row 5: Ch 1, 1 dc in next 3 sts, 1 ss in next 3 sts, 1 dc in next 2 sts, 1 ss in next st. (9 sts)

Fasten off and weave in the end tail inside the ear. Leave the starting tail for sewing.

LEFT EAR:
Using col 1 and 8mm hook, ch 7.

Row 1 (RS): 2 dc in 2nd ch from hook, 1 dc in next 5 sts. (7 sts)
Row 2: Ch 1, 1 dc in next 4 sts, 1 htr in next 3 sts. (7 sts)
Row 3: Ch 2 (does not count as st), 1 tr in first st, 1 htr in next 2 sts, 1 dc in next 3 sts, 2 dc in next st. (8 sts)
Row 4: Ch 1, 2 dc in 1st st, 1 dc in next 4 sts, 1 htr in next 3 sts. (9 sts)
Row 5: 1 ss in 1st st, 1 dc in next 2 sts, 1 ss in next 3 sts, 1 dc in next 3 sts. (9 sts)

Fasten off and weave in the end tail inside the ear. Leave the starting tail for sewing. Each ear should measure around 9cm (3½in) wide x 10cm (4in) high at the widest points.

ATTACHING EARS TO THE HEAD

Thread the starting tail of the left ear on to a yarn needle. Start counting from the point where the colourful top finishes and the head starts on the left-hand side (facing front of the toy). Skip 1st 2 sts on the head and start sewing on the left ear by making whip stitches through the starting chain of the ear and 6 following ss of the seam on the head. Skip next 10 ss on the head and sew on the right ear using starting tail to the following 6 sts. Fasten off and weave in the ends securely inside the ears.

TRUNK

The trunk is crocheted in a spiral round.

Using col 1 and 8mm hook, make a magic ring or ch 2 and work into 1st ch.
Row 1 (RS): Work 6 dc in the ring or into 2nd ch from hook. (6 sts)
Row 2: 1 dc in back loop of next 6 sts. (6 sts)
Row 3: 1 dc in next 6 sts. Flip to WS, tighten the magic ring and weave in the starting tail, flip back to RS. (6 sts)
Row 4: 1 dc in next 2 sts, 2 dc in next 2 sts, 1 dc in next 2 sts. (8 sts)
Row 5: Dc2tog, 2 dc in next 4 sts, dc2tog. (10 sts)
Row 6: Dc2tog, 1 dc in next st, 2 dc in next 4 sts, 1 dc in next st, dc2tog. (12 sts)
Row 7: Dc2tog, 1 dc in next 10 sts. Do NOT cut off the yarn. (11 sts)

Do NOT fasten off yet. Attach the next 3 sts of the trunk to the middle 3 sts on the top lip of the elephant's mouth with ss (detailed instruction below). Trunk is around 8cm (3in) long.

ATTACHING TRUNK TO THE HEAD

Insert crochet hook in the FLO of next st on the trunk. Skip 1st 3 sts on the top opening of the mouth (facing the legs of the elephant) and insert your hook in the FLO of the 4th st, yoh and pull through both sts finishing the first joining ss. Make another 2 joining ss through following 2 sts on the trunk and the top lip. Once you joined all 3 sts together, cut the yarn leaving around 38cm (15in) tail and pull your hook all the way up unravelling the working loop. Thread the yarn end on to the needle and proceed with sewing the rest of the trunk to the head (just underneath the eyes) by making overcast sts through front loops of the trunk and catching the surface of the sts on the head. Around half way through, stuff the trunk with around 2-3 grams (0.07-0.1 oz) of toy stuffing. Once you get to the starting point, weave in the remaining end inside the trunk.
(See Fig 2.)

LEGS (MAKE 4)

The legs are crocheted in a spiral round.
Using col 1 and 8mm hook, make a magic ring or ch 2 and work in 1st ch.
Rnd 1 (RS): Work 6 dc into the ring or into 2nd ch from hook. (6 sts)
Rnd 2: 2 dc in next 6 sts. Flip to WS, tighten the magic ring and weave in the starting tail, flip back to RS. (12 sts)
Rnd 3: (Dc2tog, 1 dc in next 2 sts) 3 times. (9 sts)
Rnd 4: (Dc2tog, 1 dc in next st) 3 times. (6 sts)
Rnd 5: 1 dc in each st. (6 sts)

Fasten off leaving around 30cm (12in) tail. Stuff each leg with around 1g (0.04oz) of the toy stuffing. Thread the yarn tail on yarn needle and close the opening of the leg flat, by making 3 overcast sts. Keep the remaining end for sewing the legs to the body. Each leg should be around 6cm (2½in) long.
(See Fig 3.)

ATTACHING LEGS TO THE BODY

Thread the yarn tail on yarn needle and sew on each leg to the joining seam of the body by using whip stitch. Start counting from the point where the head finishes and the colourful top starts. Skip 1st 2 sts and sew on the first leg to next 3 sts, skip next 9 sts and sew on the 2nd leg to next 3 sts, skip next 7 sts and sew on the 3rd leg to next 3 sts, skip another 9 sts and sew on the 4th leg to next 3 sts. Weave in the remaining ends in the legs.

HAIR

Cut 4 to 5 pieces of col 4, around 5cm (2in) long. Thread each piece of yarn through a needle then through the seam on the top of the head in various places, close to each other. Tie two ends of each piece of yarn into two knots to secure them. (See Fig 4.)

Fig 2

Fig 3

Fig 4

Titles also available from

978-1-912918-01-0

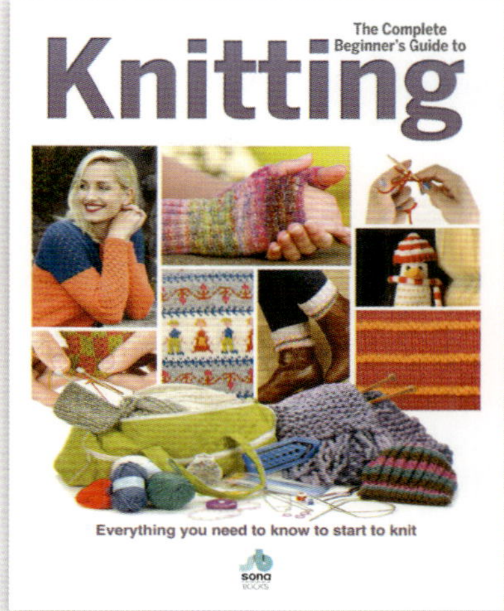

978-1-912918-02-7

978-1-912918-10-2

978-1-912918-11-9